EMERGING PROCESS:

ADVENTUROUS THEOLOGY FOR
A MISSIONAL CHURCH

Bruce G. Epperly

Parson's Porch
Books
Cleveland, TN

EMERGING PROCESS:

ADVENTUROUS THEOLOGY FOR A MISSIONAL CHURCH

Bruce G. Epperly

Parson's Porch Books

To order additional copies of this book, contact:

Parson's Porch & Company
1-423-475-7308
www.parsonsporch.com

Table of Contents

Words of Gratitude and Affirmation

LIFE-GIVING THEOLOGY EMERGES FROM our evolving personal and communal experiences of divine inspiration amid the dynamic interdependence of life. Emerging process theology arises from the faithful and ongoing gifts of a lively community of friends and colleagues. Each moment of experience and one's whole lifetime emerges from the universe and God who gives birth to all things. Accordingly, the emergence of this text in emerging process theology owes its existence to many named and unnamed persons to whom I want to give thanks. First, I am grateful to the wise persons who first introduced me to the insights of process theology and philosophy – Richard Keady and Marie Fox in the Religion and Philosophy departments, respectively, of San Jose State University and John Cobb, David Griffin, and Bernard Loomer at Claremont Graduate University. I am grateful to John Akers, pastor of Grace Baptist Church, with whom I first studied process theology in the early 1970's. These way-showers enabled me to take the first steps in my own evolving adventure in integrating process theology and Christian faith. I am grateful for the inspiration of friends and colleagues I first met in the mid-1970's at Claremont Graduate University, and whose own theological insights and evolution have shaped my own

9

evolving understanding of process theology, most especially Jay McDaniel, Catherine Keller, Rebecca Parker, and Rita Nakashima Brock. Though often separated by geography, we have been spiritually joined in a process of creating new ways to experience and articulate process theology and progressive Christianity. I am also grateful to my students in process theology and emerging Christianity at Lancaster Theological Seminary as well as two insightful and forward-looking seminary leaders, Dean Edwin Aponte and President Riess Potterveld. I thank George Hermanson and Suzanne Sykes who have provided a platform for exploring emerging process theology with participants in the Madawaska Institute, Burnstown, Ontario. I have been also inspired by companions on the way, whose questions and trust in my insights have enabled me to be a better theologian and spiritual guide, most especially, Anna Rollins, Patricia Adams Farmer, Kathy Harvey Nelson, Jo Ann Goodson, Tripp Fuller, Helene Russell, Monica Coleman, Susan Hermanson, our son Matt Epperly and his life partner Ingrid, and the community of faith at Disciples United Community Church in Lancaster, Pennsylvania. This book also emerges in creative dialogue with emerging Christians such as Brian McLaren, Jonny and Jenny Baker, Doug Pagitt, Marcus Borg, Rob Bell, Tony Jones, Diana Butler Bass, Bruce Sanguin, and Philip Newell whose words both written and spoken have been a source of ongoing inspiration. Younger theologians such as Tripp Fuller and Brian Brandsmeir have also been companions on the journey.

Through it all, Kate Epperly has been my companion and partner in marriage, ministry, parenting, and theological reflection since 1978. Together, we have lived spirit-centered process theology and progressive Christianity as pastors, workshop leaders, reiki teachers, consultants, and companions in joining the adventures of ideas with the surprising adventures of our always emerging companionship. As partners in ministry, we have explored what emerging process theology means in the context of the growth of an intimate and inspiring progressive congregation. To all these friends and colleagues, named and unnamed, I give thanks, "I am becoming because you are becoming, too."

Finally, I dedicate this text to my grandson Jack Everett Epperly for whom each day is a growing edge. May it always be so for him and his generation, who entered the world in 2010. May the world always be a beautiful place for him as the older generations reclaim their mission to heal the earth.

As you venture into this text, look toward the growing edge! Embrace the many-faceted adventure of new ideas! Awaken to the adventure of the spirit inspiring and breathing through your life. Listen for God's lively and ever-creative voice within your voice and God's moment by moment inspiration in your unique inspiration and creativity. Color outside the lines as you claim your role as God's partner in birthing new theological visions and spiritual practices.

May all who read these words experience God's ever-present vision of possibilities, intimately emerging in each moment and in every encounter. May you experience the insights of process theology in body, mind, and spirit. New worlds are being born! Look toward the growing edge!

Introduction

Emerging Process

ALL AROUND US WORLDS ARE DYING and new worlds are being born; All around us life is dying and life is being born. . . The birth of a child – life's most dramatic answer to death – This is the growing edge incarnate.

Look well to the growing edge![1]

Every blade of grass has an angel that bends over it and whispers, "Grow, grow." (A saying from the Talmud)

With the coming of each June, I scan the lawns and gardens in my Lancaster, Pennsylvania neighborhood as I take my evening walk. I look with anticipation, wondering whether or not the fireflies will return again this year. I know the fragility of the ecosystem from which fireflies emerge and the impact of global climate change, street lights, and pesticides on their survival. But, oh how I rejoice when I glimpse the first firefly's flickering light on a warm June evening! Hope is birthing, new life arising, resurrection happening, all when it's least expected and most tentative- when fragile

---

[1] Howard Thurman, *The Growing Edge* (Richmond, IN: Friends United Press,1956), 180.

13

fireflies' blinking witnesses to life's tenacious and emerging adventurousness. Look well to the growing edge! Awaken to the revelation of fireflies! Arise, shine, for your light has come! God's glory is all around you!

Today, many North American Christians are scanning the horizons for signs of emergence, glimpses of resurrection and rebirth in their congregations and denominations. The covers of major religious and secular magazines suggest that North American Christianity as we have known it for the past century may be dying. These magazine articles assert that North American Christianity is losing the vitality and vision that gave birth to a global faith two millennia ago. Many commentators rightly note that the cultural dominance once accorded to mainline Christianity has been eclipsed by the emergence of countless local and global spiritual paths available to twenty-first century seekers. These religious pundits claim that the best days of North American Christianity in all its forms are over and all we can look forward to is diminished impact, vitality, and relevance. North American moderate and progressive Christians lament the consistent declines in congregational and denominational membership and the growing percentage of members over 65 years of age. "Where are the youth?" they ask, as they wonder how they can meaningfully respond to the growing number of seekers and spiritual orphans whose mantra is "I'm spiritual but not religious." Pastors and church leaders flinch when active young adults, raised in the church and now in their mid-twenties, note that "the church as it is has nothing to offer me and my friends."

Many moderate and progressive Christians, including myself, empathize with the growing number of seekers whose experiences of Christianity suggest that the least likely place they might look for spiritual nurture is in a church! Even in the United States where religious beliefs still provoke controversies surrounding abortion rights, physician-aided death, and teaching evolution in public schools, the impact of Christianity on the overall population is rapidly diminishing. The media spotlights televangelists, new age spiritual guides, and eclectic physicians with virtually no theological training as representative of the best spiritual thinking on the problem of evil, the power of prayer, the quest for healing, and guidance for personal transformation. With few exceptions, progressive and moderate Christian leaders are seldom asked to be part of the conversation. Sadly, in the public arena Pat Robertson, Joel Osteen, Rick Warren, Benny Hinn, and Joyce Meyer are identified with the best North American Christianity has to offer. As we look at the face of North American spirituality, many of us ask "Where are the voices of progressive and open-spirited evangelical spirituality in the public square or in the spiritual marketplace?" Perhaps, more critically, we ask "What is our mission in a world in which we have been pushed from Main Street to a side street in social impact?"

Outside the church doors, seekers embark on adventures looking for world views that make sense and practices that give them peace and direction amid the ever-changing complexities of twenty-first century living. Some seekers still hope for a guiding and healing word from Christians, a spiritual signpost to guide them through the dizzying challenges and changes we face today. Many of these pilgrims enter churches, looking for spiritual nourishment and leave unsatisfied, unable to encounter the bread of life for which they so desperately yearn. Yet, many people are also discovering that spiritual practices, lacking any connection with tradition or community, are unable to provide more than superficial spiritual nourishment in their quest for an ongoing and evolving sense of the holy. Many seekers, in times of personal challenge, discover that they need a spiritual tribe, an ongoing community that gathers regularly for prayer, learning, support, and friendship. In their search for wholeness, they have discovered that spiritual workshops and self help books alone cannot provide the ongoing nurture found in loving arms, listening ears, and caring challenges.

"Worlds are dying," noted Howard Thurman. In words addressed to contemporary North American Christians, Canadian theologian Douglas John Hall asserts that the future we anticipate and toward which we work can no longer be the future of old.[2] Given the demise of Christendom, the world in which Christianity was at the heart of political, cultural and spiritual life of believers and unbelievers alike, Hall notes that we can either be passive victims or energetic artists of the spirituality of the future. Hall counsels Christians, both individually and in

---

[2]Douglas John Hall, *The End of Christendom and the Future of Christianity* (Eugene, Oregon: Wipf and Stock Publishers, 1997), ix.

community, to create new, lively, and evolving futures out of the disestablishment of Christendom. Hall asks persons still dedicated to the pathway of Jesus: "whether we will simply allow the process of disestablishment to happen to us or whether, as individuals or Christian bodies, we will take some active part in directing the process." [3] Will we deny the eclipse of Christendom or passively await its demise? Or, will we, as the philosopher Alfred North Whitehead notes, originate novelties to match the novelties of our environment? [4] To put it another way, will we trust the yearly witness of fireflies who, despite their fragility and environmental threats, emerge each summer as a sign of hope and inspiration for persons who seek new pathways for spiritual transformation? Will we discover God's growing edge quietly emerging amid signs of death and destruction?

Just for a moment, I invite you to put down the text, and consider God's growing edge as it relates to Christian faith in the twenty-first century. Take a few minutes to reflect on your vision of the future of Christianity's vocation in the world being born. What future do you imagine for moderate and progressive Christianity today? What images of hope emerge as you ponder what lies ahead for you on your spiritual journey? What images of hope inspire you as you consider the future of our planet? Where might Christian

---

[3] Ibid., 39.

[4]

Alfred North Whitehead, *Process and Reality: Corrected Edition.* Edited by David Ray Griffin and Donald Sherburne. (New York: Free Press, 1978), 102.

communities become catalysts for creative transformation and global healing in the years ahead? Where do intuit God's emerging mission for you personally and for your congregation or fellowship group? What might you do to share in God's growing edge?

This book was born of a sense of mission and urgency. As theologian and pastor who has been active in the training of laypeople, seminarians, and pastors for over thirty years, I believe that neither the pathway of *denial,* characterized by the authoritative pronouncements of religious fundamentalists, nor the pathway *passivity,* reflected in the predictions of naysayers within once mainstream Christianity, can creatively respond to the ever-increasing cultural, political, and spiritual novelties of our time. I believe that lively spiritual transformation takes another path – a pathway embracing novelty, living with contrasting viewpoints, and recognizing the constantly shifting spiritual landscape – as the inspiration from which we initiate novelty to respond to the novelties of our world.

The path of creative and life-giving transformation looks toward the growing edge, mindfully anticipating the return of the firefly. It rejoices in the emergence of fragile spirit-centered communities of faith that celebrate pluralism, hospitality, and creativity in worship, spiritual practices, and theological reflection.

In the midst of the death of old worlds, Thurman proclaims that "new worlds are being born." This is my hope and the hope many imaginative Christians and seekers today. New and creative spiritualities and theologies are emerging, more often in house churches and fragile faith communities than in big steeple churches, seminaries and, denominational church offices.[5] I believe that in this time of lively, grassroots emergence, where old barriers between liberal and conservative, action and contemplation, and lay and clergy no longer apply, an emerging and progressive process-oriented theology gives voice to an alternative vision of the future of Christianity.[6] This phoenix vision of a vital emerging and

---

[5]

Among the most insightful books in emerging or emergent Christianity are: Tony Jones, *The New Christians: Dispatches from the Emergent Frontier* (New York: Jossey-Bass, 2009); Brian McLaren, *A New Kind of Christian* (San Francisco: Jossey-Bass, 2001) , *A Generous Orthodoxy* (Grand Rapids: Zondervan, 2004), and *A New Kind of Christianity* (New York: Harper, 2010); Doug Pagitt, *A Christianity Worth Believing* (San Francisco: Jossey-Bass, 2008); Bruce Sanguin, *The Emerging Church*(Kelowa, British Columbia: Copper House, 2008).

[6]

Process theology is grounded in the work of Alfred North Whitehead and Charles Hartshorne. Some of the major works in process thought include: Alfred North Whitehead, *Process and Reality* (New York:Macmillan, 1929 [Corrected Edition, 1978]); *Religion in the Making* (New York: Macmillan, 1926); and *Adventures of Ideas* (New York: Macmillan, 1933); Charles Hartshorne, *The Divine Relativity* (New Haven: Yale University Press, 1982) and *Creative Synthesis and Philosophic Method* (Chicago: Open Court Publishing Company, 1970); John Cobb, *A Christian Natural Theology* (Philadelphia: Westminster Press, 1965) and *Christ in a Pluralistic Age* (Louisville: Westminster/John Knox, 1975).

19

agile faith arises from a spirit-centered and evangelically-passionate progressive Christianity. A vital and emerging process-oriented theology embraces the past, but looks toward the horizon of God's future. Emerging paths of theology and spiritual practice are guided by a flexible and evolving vision of the God and the world. Its commitment to following God's surprising revelations, wherever they take us awakens us to novelty and transformation and wholeness and holiness amid the complex realities of personal and cultural transformation. This emerging theological vision welcomes pluralism and novelty in light of its own protean, shape-shifting, and lively vision of faith, grounded in the affirmation of a shape-shifting, ever-changing, ever-faithful Holy Adventurer whose movements in our world inspire the transformation in persons and in planets. God is constantly doing new things, and calling us to do likewise. As I look at the current malaise in once mainstream Christianity, I believe that process theology provides a vision of reality and spiritual practices that can energize and guide a robust progressive faith in its mission for the twenty-first century.

I am by training and affirmation a process theologian, whose vocation is to midwife the birth of a new kind of progressive, process-oriented theology, liberated from the narrow confines of academic institutions and the irrelevance of abstract philosophical language so that it might become a voice for creative transformation among emerging Christian communities, traditional congregations, and the growing number of persons who call themselves "spiritual but not religious."

I believe that an emerging process theology has the potential of bursting through the "old wineskins" of theological reflection and doctrinal certainty to provide the "new wine" of affirmation, celebration, and transformation in the uncertain days of the twenty-first century. In the spirit of emerging church leader Brian McLaren, process theology proclaims a new vision of God and the world as inspirational for a "new kind of Christian" and a "new kind of Christianity." Though the words of Alfred North Whitehead and his theological followers describe the intellectual and theological landscape of process theology, emerging process theology is holistic in nature, intended to be personally experienced and to be the heart of a practice-oriented way of life, embracing person and planet. More than words for theological hair-splitting and doctrinal argumentation, an emerging process theology fosters a way of life that transforms people and heals the world. Its goal is to enable us to emerge as responsible and active partners in the creation of God's holy adventure in our midst. Despite its awkwardness, I will use the term "emerging process theology" throughout this text interchangeably with the more familiar "process theology" as a description of the fact that process theology itself is being creatively transformed in light of the emerging and progressive spiritual movements of our time.

As the co-pastor of an emerging, progressive congregation in Lancaster, Pennsylvania for several years, I have seen the power of a lively emerging process theology and spirituality to transform persons' lives and provide a way in which people can be both spiritual and religious. I have seen process theology's ability to bring healing to people wrestling with out-worn images of God, intellectual dualisms, guilt and shame, and questions of sexual identity.

I believe that a vital and emerging process theology can serve as a creative and liberating theological movement for the growing number of emerging spiritual leaders of all age groups, who are venturing beyond narrow doctrines and confining institutionalism to imagine new forms of mission. Emerging process theology can provide a vision and pathway for faithfully and creatively embracing the challenges of postmodernism.

More than just an intellectual exercise, emerging process theology, unlike much postmodern theology, can be lived out in your personal and corporate life. Living process theology – that is, experiencing the insights of process theology in your whole being, in your cells, sinews, and touch - dynamically joins spiritual experience, theological reflection, and life-transforming action in ways that can enable Christians and other seekers to respond faithfully and flexibly to the spiritual, ethical, and intellectual challenges that Christians and seekers alike face. In so doing, spiritually vital progressive Christians and their open-spirited evangelical companions will discover life-giving resources for giving birth to faithful and creative ways of sharing the pathway of Jesus in our time. They may discover that beyond a de-centered Christendom is the reality that God's center is everywhere and divine inspiration touches all creation.

Emerging Process and the Promise of Postmodernism.[7] The pervasive impact of postmodernism in its many forms, both culturally and spiritually, can either be theologically devastating or spiritually transforming. The deconstruction of all global stories, the suspicion of abstract metaphysics, and the emphasis on locality and personal experience as sources of living truths can be frightening to those who seek infallible proof for their faith tradition's superiority and insist on the inferiority of other pathways to the divine. Postmodern thinkers rightly insist that infallible proof, available to all rational beings, is an illusion that prevents us from experiencing the surprising realities within which we live, move, and have our being. Postmodern thinkers also insist that pluralism of our time challenges the authority of any universally-held world views or scriptural texts. Postmodern sages remind us that Buddhists, Christians, and Muslims alike proclaim the uniqueness and superiority of their own tradition's vision of ultimate reality and human life. While recognizing that doctrines and world views can positively shape our daily lives and character, postmodernism also reminds us that creeds and doctrines reflect the ongoing faith experiences and traditions of finite and localized communities and cannot

---

[7]For exploring postmodernism from a Christian perspective, see John Caputo, *What Would Jesus Deconstruct* (Grand Rapids, MI: Baker Books, 2007); Peter Rollins, *How (Not) to Speak About God* (Brewster, MA: Paraclete Press, 2006) and *The Fidelity of Betrayal: Towards a Church Beyond Belief* (Brewster, MA: Paraclete Press, 2008).

be applied to every culture or human being. The apostolic faith "once for all" delivered to the saints is, in fact, being transformed in the context of each new generation's dialogue with its cultural, religious, and technological context. Holding fast to any doctrine as universal and infallible stifles creativity, mysticism, and questioning, and closes the door to the Life-giving Spirit that freely moves throughout the universe.

Such postmodern proclamations witness to the death knell of absolutism in all its forms, even though fundamentalists of all faith traditions continue to proclaim vociferously the uniqueness and superiority of their religious points of view. Parochial religious proclamations become all the more suspect to today's spiritual seekers, whose global quests lead them to life-changing encounters with Christians, Buddhists, Hindus, Muslims, and new agers, many of whom also proclaim the authority and inspiration and, in many cases, the universality and superiority of their competing scriptures, channeled documents, and understandings of salvation. When rigidly held religious beliefs lead to oppression, violence, exclusion, and war-making, the spiritual credibility of religious fundamentalism and doctrinal exclusivism becomes even more suspect to spiritual seekers.

In contrast to rigidly held and universally applicable statements of faith, I believe a lively and emerging process vision grounds itself in the dynamic interplay of the *apophatic* and *kataphatic* approaches to theology. In the spirit of *apophatic* theology, I recognize that nothing fully reveals the holy. God is always more than we imagine; the divine horizon recedes even as we perceive ourselves moving closer to it. This is good news! For God's holy adventure exceeds our wildest dreams and calls us to our own personal and community holy adventures into God's Great Mystery. Still, in the spirit of *kataphatic* theology, our experiences and words for God are also revealing; all things may become vehicles of experiencing holiness and wholeness in our time and place. This is also good news! For we can experience God's healing touch and liberating visions even if we can barely describe them. As the apostle Paul asserted in his own pluralistic age, we have this treasure – our experience of God, our way of life, our vision of reality, and our faithful practices – in earthen vessels, that is, in our temporary, limited, and evolving perspectives on reality. (2 Corinthians 4:7) We can affirm our faith tradition's life-transforming treasures, but the incomparable wisdom of our faith tradition always emerges from the unique interplay of the divine and human call and response in our personal and community lives. As the apostle Paul also notes, we will always look through a mirror dimly in our quest to experience the holy. (1 Corinthians 13:12) Spirituality and theology are most faithful to the Adventurous God when they, like our lively experiences of God, are also protean, creative, and constantly emerging themselves. When we let go of the "perfect" theological or spiritual perspective, we discover world views and spiritual practices that are "good enough" to inspire, transform, and heal ourselves and the world.

For spirit-centered progressive and process theologians, spiritual leaders, and pilgrims, who seek experiences of holiness and wholeness that shape our lives and visions of reality, the promise of postmodernism inspires the transformation and revitalization of theology through the affirmation of the spiritual experiences of people everywhere, including mystical encounters with the holy; local, communal, and personal visions of God; the affirmation of multiple ways to experience and describe the divine; and lively communal and personal testimonies and confessions of faith. This is truly good news that foreshadows the birth of new faith worlds! Faith arises in tasting and seeing God's goodness in celebrative meals and the grandeur of nature, hearing the voice of God in a companion's testimony, smelling the holiness of clear mountain air or incense in worship, working diligently for planetary and neighborhood healing, and touching God energetically through laying on of hands and reiki healing touch. Indeed, the promise of postmodernism is found in the affirmation of our experiences and witnesses to God's movements in our lives. Each of us has a vantage point on the divine that we can share with others as we grow together through affirming one another's spiritual quests.

My vision for this text is that it will open the doors of progressive Christianity and process theology to new and emerging movements of God's Spirit and new ways of embodying its wisdom in everyday life and the social and planetary quests for healing and justice. I believe that process theology's mission is to be catalytic in transforming and energizing of an open-spirited progressive and mission-oriented Christian faith in our postmodern world. In this transformative process, process theology will also be transformed and renewed. While we cannot universalize the insights of process theology, we can affirm these insights as inspiring and insightful approaches to creatively experiencing God's movements in the permanent whitewater world in which we live. Process theology provides pathways for encountering God, creating holistic spiritual practices, and awakening to the wisdom of God in the many voices of faith. Process theology comes alive in our experiences of holiness and wholeness, and can serve as a life-transforming pathway toward a dynamic, spirit-centered, and emerging Christianity, fragile as each year's returning fireflies yet as persistent as the growing edge that brings forth new faith forms in a time of searching and uncertainty.

Chapter One

Living Process Theology

Religions commit suicide when they find their inspirations in their dogmas. The inspiration of religion lies in the history of religion.

By this I mean that it is found in the primary expressions of the intuitions of religious lives. The sources of religious belief are always growing, though some supreme expressions may lie in the past.[8]

THE SOURCES OF RELIGIOUS FAITH ARE always growing. God never stands still, nor should we in shaping our imperfect, but emerging, visions of God and the universe. Today's spiritual seekers are in quest of a new kind of faith and new kind of spirituality. They are also looking for an alternative vision of God, one that embraces the beauty of the earth, welcomes diversity, and supports creativity. If God is to be relevant at all to those who are spiritual but not religious, persons of faith must describe

---

[8] Alfred North Whitehead, *Religion in the Making,* 138.

God in ways that reflect love rather than coercion and affirmation rather than punishment.

Although I have told this story before, it bears repeating because it reflects the dawning of my own theological journey; the discovery that the God of my childhood faith was too small to contain the love I felt for a four footed friend. When I was five years old, my brother Bill and I were left under the watchful eye a pious Baptist lady while my parents attended a church convention. The highpoint of my time was falling in love with her fox terrier Taffy as we played in the shadow of the majestic Morro Rock on California's Pacific Coast. It was truly boy meets dog season.

Being a pious Baptist child, I was inspired to inquire about the eternal soul of my canine companion. "Will Taffy go to heaven?" I asked. She paused a moment, and frowned as if I'd committed one of the seven deadly sins, before she snapped back, "Don't you dare ask such a question! You better talk with your father. Hasn't he told you that dogs don't go to heaven? Don't you know that God only loves humans and Jesus only died for our sins!" I felt stunned, embarrassed, and ashamed. But, something else burst forth in my experience. I also felt anger – at this pious Baptist lady and at the God she described. At that moment, my childhood image of a loving God was shaken and the first seeds of a great theological adventure were sown. Even though I had no words to describe my experience, deep down I knew I could no longer believe in a God who had no place for fox terriers in heaven. Within a decade, I was a full-fledged spiritual refugee, whose emerging faith no longer fit within the narrow confines of small-spirited Baptist theology by which I was raised.

Recently, I had a similar experience at the Pride Fest in Lancaster, Pennsylvania. As I walked by one of the bible-quoting hecklers, I commented ironically, "May God forgive you," to which he quickly replied, "You and I have different gods!" As I walked away, I considered his comment. Perhaps he was right. Perhaps we believe in different gods, or at least very different visions of God and God's relationship to diverse human and the non-human world. In such moments of challenge and dissonance, we discover that theology really matters. We discover the reality that even if all theologies are imperfect and limited, still what we believe shapes how we view the environment, the destiny of non-humans, issues of sexual identity, and our responsibility for shaping our lives and the future of the planet.

Postmodern thinkers remind liberal and conservative Christians and seekers alike that each one of us sees the world through certain theological, spiritual, sociological, and experiential lenses. Although none of these lenses gives us universal and infallible vision, these theological lenses shape what we see and how we interpret the events of our lives. These lenses are so intimately connected with our personal and group identity that we often assume that reality is exactly as we experience or describe it and that only our community's vision portrays God and human life accurately.

Our personal interpretations of reality – shaped by the lenses through which we see the world - arise from many factors such as: cultural context, historical location, family of origin, personal chemistry, ethnic experience, unconscious memory, level of education, social and political context, and faith tradition. Our communal, denominational, and faith tradition images of reality also arise from a constellation of historical, cultural, ethnic, philosophical, experiential and scientific factors. While emerging process theologians recognize that we cannot make absolute judgments about our own or other faith traditions' visions of reality, we can realize that some visions of reality are healthy and life-affirming, while others diminish our sense of value, limit our possibilities, and alienate us from God, nature, our bodies, and other persons. The challenge for spiritual seekers and theologians is to experience and then describe God's presence in our world as broadly and clearly as possible in the context of the gifts and limitations of our time, place, and history.

Still, despite the particularity of every theological faith vision, I believe that healthy and life-supporting religious traditions and theological perspectives provide us with:

- A comprehensive life-orienting and life-changing *vision* or picture of reality which enables us to discover pathways to meaning and wholeness, especially in the context of challenge, change, and conflict.
- A *promise* that we can experience the world as described by our vision of reality and in so doing experience wholeness and joy amid the complexities of life.

31

· *Spiritual and ethical* practices that enable us to experience the life-changing and meaning-giving realities that our faith tradition or theology describes.

Put simply, a person's or a community's deeply-held visions of God and the world shape our character, inspire a sense of meaning, and encourage life-transforming spiritual practices and behaviors. This is true for every theological standpoint, including emerging process theology. Process theologians believe that God is present in our lives and that we can experience God's presence more deeply and concretely through the integration of theological reflection, spiritual practice, life-changing action, and the commitment to constantly measure our vision of reality in light of the dynamic world we experience and our encounters with diverse religious, philosophical, and cultural perspectives.

Just take a moment to reflect upon your life: how does your vision of God or image of the future shape your day to day life? Does it inspire hope and activism, or despair and passivity? How does it influence your response to negative events, whether in your personal health or in the economy? Do you believe that all the important details of your life been determined by God, your family of origin, or your DNA, or do you believe that you have the freedom to change your life and play a role in the future of our planet? Does your vision of God influence how you respond to issues such as global climate change, physician-aided death, and cloning?

Your answers to these questions can lead to health or sickness and life or death, for yourself and the larger environment.

The philosophical parent of process theology Alfred North Whitehead once noted that our understandings of reality shape our day to day decisions and character over the long haul.[9] A student of mine at Central Michigan University once told the story of a conversation with a farmer who hired him to paint his home. After finishing the first coat of paint, he asked the farmer if he should do another coat and caulk the windows. The farmer replied, "Don't bother to do anything else; Jesus is coming soon!" Since that time in 1981, there have a lot of cold Michigan winters and I suspect that the farmer is rather disappointed at the delay in Jesus' return!

While this story represents a humorous perspective on the impact of religious beliefs on our personal behavior, there are many tragic and politically dangerous examples of religious beliefs that lead to death rather than life, both for persons and communities. About the same time as the Michigan farmer deferred necessary home improvements, I read an article claiming that James Watt, the USA Secretary of Interior, serving under President Ronald Reagan, advocated opening protected government lands to business enterprises, partly because he believed that the time was short before Jesus' return and the subsequent destruction of the earth! He believed that

---

[9] Alfred North Whitehead, *Religion in the Making*, 15.

there was no reason to save forests and open spaces that soon would be destroyed by a divinely-ordained cataclysm. Ironically, despite his belief in the imminent return of Jesus, the Secretary saw no reason to prohibit corporate and personal profit-making from these same government lands! Conservative Christian skepticism about the realities of global climate change, like its opposition to teaching evolution in public schools in the United States, is not accidental but based on theological viewpoints characterized by: 1) antagonism to science, 2) the belief that the destruction of the earth is essential to God's plan of salvation, and 3) the affirmation that what interferes with the free market also stands in the way of God's will. While the USA Constitution prohibits the establishment of any particular faith tradition, it is clear that what politicians and voters believe can lead to acts of justice, as in the case of Civil Rights Acts, or to denial of equal rights to gay and lesbian persons.

Beliefs about the nature of revelation and authority can cure or kill. Pastors have encouraged battered spouses to stay in marriages because they believe that divorce is a sin and women are commanded to honor and obey their husbands! Other people have refused life-saving medical treatment because they believed that going to doctors rather than directly to the Great Physician for a cure represented a lack of faith that might jeopardize their eternal destiny! Still others have experienced debilitating "new age guilt" as a result of being told that "you create your own reality and that you are totally responsible for your cancer." While the notion of "creating your own reality" can encourage personal responsibility and decision-making, more often than not it reflects the privileged status of healthy and prosperous spiritual seekers rather than impoverished or chronically ill persons who have tried every spiritual self-help recipe but still remain limited by forces beyond their control.[10]

What we believe truly matters: our faith can make us whole and be the tipping point between life and death, when we are facing a critical illness. Our faith can also motivate us to become God's partners in healing the earth, seeking justice for the impoverished, and equality for all persons regardless of gender, race, ethnicity, or sexual identity.

Life-Transforming Theology. Emerging process theology asserts that life is dynamic and mutable. Persons may experience "conversions," "great awakenings," and "enlightenments." We can change our visions of reality and, thus, change our values, behaviors, and perceptions by our committed beliefs and practices. As the apostle Paul affirms, "Be not conformed to this world, but be transformed by the renewing of your mind." (Romans 12:2) Doctrines, rituals, community support, and daily faith practices shape – and transform – our images of reality and eventually our actions. We think ourselves into new behaviors and act ourselves into new beliefs!

---

[10] For more about the relationship of Christianity and the new age movement, see Bruce Epperly, *Crystal and Cross: Christians and the New Age in Creative Dialogue* (Mystic, CT: Twenty-third Publications, 1996).

Transformed theological affirmations can lead to transformed lives and experiences of the divine.

Recently, in a conversation with a friend of my mine who was diagnosed with breast cancer and lymphoma, our son Matt, himself a cancer survivor, described himself as "loosely Christian." At first glance, the words of this thirty year old young professional may sound threatening to those who live by the doctrinal certainties of the "old time religion." Perhaps, they might even question the depth of my commitment to Christ as a parent, given the fact that my wife Kate and I raised Matt in a deeply Christian, but pluralistic and radically affirming faith context, in which questions were welcomed and in which lived experience and ethics more authentically reflected the way of Jesus than adherence to ancient creeds or abstract doctrines. Nevertheless, I have come to believe that Matt's self-description expresses not only the best of young adult theology, but also the heart of emerging process Christianity. In a time of religious and theological pluralism and upheaval, we need to be "loosely Christian," affirming ancient wisdom but opening to new visions of God and the world. In a world that changes nanosecond by nanosecond, we need lively, dynamic, tentative, inclusive, and agile faith visions, big enough to be cosmic and intimate enough to be personal.

The spirit of emerging process theology reflects a conversation I had with another friend, who related a dream in which his conservative Christian mother, now deceased, confessed that "Christianity is different than I thought it was." For those who see Christianity as narrow, backward looking, and tied to the past, emerging

36

process theology claims that God is on the move and so should be our theological perspectives! Emerging process theology invites us to claim our` faith again as if for the first time!

As a resource for the emerging Christianity of the future, process theology affirms a uniquely lively and relational progressive vision of Christian faith, reflecting a creative and dynamic interplay of scripture, Christian tradition, reason, experience, and the best cultural thinking and science of our time. In fact, process theology affirms the traditional Wesleyan quadrilateral, plus one other factor, the dynamic and emerging insights and technological advances of culture as a fifth source of divine revelation and religious reflection. Process theology also invites us to explore reality in terms of dynamic, lively relationships that apply, in one way or another, to every possible experience, including God's. Emerging process theology is loosely Christian, unattached to any tradition and rule so that it might be faithful to the concrete and evolving pathways of Jesus.

According to the parent of modern process theology and philosophy, Alfred North Whitehead, speculative philosophy, or metaphysics, resembles the flight of an airplane: it begins on the ground with concrete experience, soars into the heights of generalization in order to gain perspective on reality as a whole, and then returns to the ground of concrete experience with new interpretations of the world.[11] Our experiences of personal transformation – of healing and

---

[11] Whitehead, *Process and Reality,* 5

growth – point to deeper, more pervasive realities that shape the emergence of communities, congregations, families, and planets. Though we can never fully fathom God's nature, our lives witness to – and provide evidence for – a movement toward wholeness and beauty – amid the complexity of an evolving universe.

Emerging Process Affirmations. The words "process-relational" describe the heart of this lively and inspirational vision of reality. Initially articulated by thinkers such as Alfred North Whitehead, Charles Hartshorne, Bernard Loomer and later by theologians such as John Cobb, Schubert Ogden, Marjorie Suchocki, and David Griffin, process theology makes the following affirmations about the world in which we live:

- *Relationship is primary and essential to reality.* We are not isolated atomic individuals. Rather, each moment of our lives emerges from our unique experience of our environment. The environment, including each momentary occasion's most recent personal past, in the case of humans, is the material out of which each occasion "creates" its immediate experience and gift to the future. The interdependence of life applies to all things, divine, human, and non-human alike.

- *Reality is dynamic – living beings are in a constant process of creative transformation.* Experience is dynamic; no two moments in anyone's life are the same. What is unchanging in life, most importantly the influence of the past, including the life-changing impact of certain spiritual ideals, is embraced by the changing and evolving universe and the ongoing experience of God. While both eternity and process are real, process theology embraces and makes concrete the eternal within the world of change and transformation. The greater possibility for change and growth in a creature's experience, the more highly evolved that creature is: living persons are more "alive" than rocks because their complexity enables them to embrace more of reality with greater experiential insight and sensitivity. Their mutability and flexibility gives testimony both to their complexity and breadth of experience. Personal and community transformation points to the emergence of new ways of living our lives and imagining the human and planetary future.

Experience is universal, and not limited to human life. This is one of the more radical affirmations of process theology and philosophy. Existence implies some level of experience or relationship with the world, although experience does not necessarily mean consciousness. For example, a fetus unconsciously experiences her mother in terms of her ambient feeling tones and intimate nurture; a cell experiences its environment in terms of its survival and growth – it values certain things and avoids others, even though it is not self-conscious. The impact of non-conscious experience is confirmed by the growing

39

recognition that pre-natal experiences emerging from a fetus' encounter with its environment - emotional, relational, and dietary - may shape the future of a child, psychologically as well as physically. Yet, even the fetus has a degree of freedom in responding to the impact of it's the amniotic and emotional environment provided by its mother. Process thought also tells us that non-humans, whether dolphins, fireflies, cicadas, or fox terriers, also experience the world in unique ways, and, accordingly, deserve moral consideration as we weigh human incursions into the non-human world. With the Psalmist, emerging process thought affirms "let everything that breathes praise God." (Psalm 150:6) The lilies of the field and the birds of the air not only testify to God's aim at beauty but are living revelations of divine wisdom, often more convincing than theological tomes. (Matthew 6:25-34)

· *Experience and value are intimately related.* Although Whitehead notes, that "life is robbery" and involves the destruction for less complex creatures to insure the survival and flourishing of more complex creatures, our recognition of the pervasive reality of experience calls us to affirm what Albert Schweitzer described as reverence for life. Although rocks and trees lack centers of experience that join their various cells and molecules under the guidance of a single organizing center of experience, they are nevertheless composed of sentient elements. They are loosely joined "societies" or "communities" of experiencing cells. Spiritually speaking, this means that we are not alone in a meaningless unfeeling universe, but part of a universe of experience, ranging from the simplest to most divine forms of experience. We do not as humans create the meaning of life, but are part of a many-layered meaning-giving universe. Ethically, it means we must give moral consideration to non-humans as well as humans.

· *Freedom is real, but conditioned.* To exist is to experience the world from a unique perspective. Each moment of experience embraces its environment, and shapes that experience in its own unrepeatable way. Even the simplest organisms have an element of novelty, despite their tendency to repeat with virtually no change what they have inherited from their environment. Every organism uniquely experiences the world in *this* place and *this* time. In each moment, we are able to choose again and again – shaping our responses to the universe in new ways, innovating to transform the world one moment at a time. Our choices constantly shape what we experience in novel and unique ways. Though our freedom as humans is always conditioned by the past, including the impact of our own past experiences as well as the impact of the world from which we emerge, we are never passive victims of our environment and past history. In this spirit, psychiatrist and parent of logotherapy Victor Frankl notes that even in Auschwitz, we have choices that can be tipping points between life and death and hope and hopelessness. Frankl asserts that "everything can be taken away from a [person] but one thing: the last of the human freedoms – to choose one's attitude in any set of circumstances, to choose one's way." [12] From an emerging process perspective, we can assert that in partnership with God, we can claim our role as agents in personal and social transformation that shapes the universe beyond ourselves. Claiming our freedom, especially when we have experienced oppression or trauma, requires a great deal of intentionality and struggle; nevertheless, we can transform the negative impact of the past through openness to divine possibility and the support of a healing community.

· *God is the primary example of the dynamic, relational, and creative nature of life.* While all descriptions of God are limited and provisional, process theologians affirm that God is not an exception to the nature of reality, but the prime example of interdependence, relationship, and creativity. The living God shapes and is shaped by

---

[12] Victor Frankl, *Man's Search for Meaning,* 65.

all things. God is not aloof, but is present in every situation, providing creative possibilities everywhere in the emerging universe. God's power is not coercive but relational in nature. God works within the lively, dynamic, relational world to bring forth the highest possibilities for freedom and creativity among creatures. God is the ultimate source of the evolutionary process, emerging over billions of years in billions of galaxies through an ongoing call and response. As the motto of the United Church of Christ proclaims, "God is still speaking." Accordingly, God is not locked in the past by God's previous choices (what orthodox followers of John Calvin describe as predestination) or limited by an unchanging foreknowledge of all things (often, I believe, inaccurately described as omniscience). In contrast to deterministic understandings of God and the world, emerging process theology asserts that God constantly adapts to the unfolding world in order to more fully inspire the world toward abundant life, justice, and beauty. Open to every influence, shaped by every creature, God freely and lovingly seeks wholeness for creation in all of its diversity and complexity.

In the chapters to come, I will explore the creative resources of emerging process theology as they relate to everyday life, religious doctrines, spiritual formation, science and medicine, worship, evangelism, and ethical decision-making. My approach will be kaleidoscopic in nature; discovering the many-faceted and colorful nature of emerging process theology with every turn of the kaleidoscope. Process theology is always growing, emerging, and inspiring new forms of reflection, ethical action, spiritual formation, and planetary responsibility. Inspired by the growing edges of life, emerging process theology is unfinished and unfinishable. Accordingly, the adventure of emerging process theology calls us to embrace novelty as well as the richness of tradition as we seek to faithful to God and to our world.

Living Process Theology

As a spiritual resource for progressive and moderate Christianity, process theology is meant to be lived not just spoken about. Accordingly, each chapter will conclude with a spiritual practice whose purpose is to invite you to experience process theology as a lived reality that can heal and transform your life. I believe that process theology arises from a dynamic and intimate call and response with an emerging and evolving God. Because God is constantly and intimately moving in our lives, I believe that personally and corporately, we have all the guidance and inspiration we need to respond moment by moment to the novelties of the day. Still, the wisdom of emerging process calls us to practice the vision we affirm. After all, "practice makes better" in our ability to live the insights of emerging process theology in every setting of life.

Grounded in our personal and communal experiences, our individual and group practices both mirror and change the world in which we live. Through intentional spiritual practices, we can consciously become partners in the emergence of new ways of experiencing and shaping ourselves in companionship with the emerging and adventurous God the future of our planet through creative spiritual practices.

Each chapter contains a practice to enable you to experience what you have just read. At the conclusion of this book, I will provide questions and spiritual practices for personal or small group study and conversation. These questions are open-ended and in the spirit of emerging process thought intended to inspire you to be a partner in the creative transformation of this text and process theology itself.

An Emerging Spiritual Practice

In this practice, simply notice the world in which you live. Process theology invites us to "live" the omnipresence of God by noticing God's movements in all things. As you go through your day, open your mind and heart to inspiration, creaturely or divine, wherever you find it. Listen for the divine voice in the many voices you hear. Awaken to God's presence in your relationships as you discover God's presence in those whom you encounter. Experience holiness in all your senses – through touch that heals, tasting the goodness of God in the foods you eat, seeing the world as an icon of the divine, hearing the harmony of the spheres, and smelling the aromas of the earth.

Aware of God's movements in all things, including your own daily life, take time to give thanks for the blessings and wonders of life.

As a prompt to group spiritual reflection, you might choose to play Carrie Newcomer's song "Holy is the Day" in which the singer-songwriter invites us to see the gentle movements of God in the woman at the checkout stand, in a sleeping dog, and in everyday tasks like folding clothes.[13]

---

[13] Carrie Newcomer, "Holy as the Day is Spent" from *A Gathering of Spirits* (2002).

Chapter Two

God of Change and Glory

God is the poet of the world, with tender patience leading it by his vision of truth, beauty, and goodness.[14]

ONE OF THE MOST MOVING WORSHIP services I've experienced was the Service of Installation for Susan Zabel as full professor at Wesley Theological Seminary. Earlier that year, Sue had been diagnosed with a form of cancer that would eventually lead to her death. She would be going on disability leave shortly after her promotion to full professor. But, the service was filled with joy – it spoke of Sue's commitment to the church, to her role as a theological educator, and to her deep trust in a God who provides no guarantees that the road will be easy, but who assures us that God will always be with us as companion, inspirer, and everlasting hope. There were few dry eyes in the seminary chapel as Sue led the gathered community in the closing hymn, Al Carmines' "God of Change and Glory." Listen to these words of witness to a never-

---

[14] Alfred North Whitehead, *Process and Reality,* 346.

ending, ever-emerging love that embraces us in every season of life.

> *God of change and glory, God of time and space,*
>
> *when we fear the future, give to us your grace.*
>
> *In the midst of changing ways, give to us the grace to praise....*
>
> *Freshness of the morning, newness of each night,*
>
> *you are still creating endless love and light.*
>
> *This we see, as shadows part, many gifts from one great heart.*
>
> *Many gifts, one Spirit, one love known in many ways.*
> *In our difference is blessing, from diversity we praise*
>
> *one Giver, one Word, one Spirit, one God known in many ways, hallowing our days. For the giver, for the gifts, praise, praise, praise!*[15]

---

[15]Al Carmines, "God of Change and Glory." Used by permission.

Imagine living in a world of praise, in which you experience God as utterly dependable, fully present, and universally supportive. Imagine the joy of knowing a God who companions persons with cancer and inspires leaders to seek justice. Such a God is truly worthy of our praise!

Process theology is best known for its life-transforming images of God. Process theologians believe that God is the primary example of the interdependence, relationship, creativity, and possibility that define the world in which we "live and move and have our being." (Acts 17-28)

As you reflect on the vision of the relational and lively God inspired by emerging process theology, I invite you to consider the following thought experiment: When you think of God, what images come to mind? How did you view God as a child? How has your vision of God changed over the years? What characteristics of divinity give you confidence? What characteristics of God raise concerns and questions?

How we imagine God is important in shaping our values, spiritual practices, and daily lives. If God is the ultimate reality, then the goal of the spiritual life is to attune ourselves to the values that are important to God. How we view God's character and activity also shapes the way we think of relationships, the appropriate use of corporate and political power, matters of health and illness, the problem of evil, the nature of truth, and how we respond to enemies, whether personal, political, or international.

Process theologians recognize that speaking about God is always challenging. The theologian Karl Barth once spoke of theological reflection about God as being similar to painting a bird in flight. Process theologian Catherine Keller describes the quest to experience and understand God as a pathway toward the mystery.[16] God is mysterious not only because God is beyond our mortal imaginations, but also because God is the Great and Holy Adventurer whose agility and creativity inspire and respond to the ever-changing world.

Do you remember Proteus, the shape-shifting sea-god of Greek mythology? Infinitely flexible and versatile, Proteus could manifest as a lion, elephant, seagull, or flying fish. When you expected Proteus to be one particular creature, he would surprise you by taking on an entirely different form. The same is surely true for the One who creatively and intimately responds to every moment of experience, becoming a "new" God to respond to the novelty of the universe.

Jewish and Christian theologians and spiritual guides have described the Living-Changing God in terms of the polarity of *apophatic* and *kataphatic*. On the one hand, no language can fully describe God, since God is beyond language and transcends our experience. On the other hand, everything points to God insofar as all of our words and experiences reveal something of the holy. Hindus capture this same theological contrast in the polarity of *nirguna* and *saguna Brahman:* Ultimate Reality as unknowable and beyond any characteristics we can imagine and Ultimate Reality as knowable and revealed in

---

[16] Catherine Keller, *Toward the Mystery: Discerning Divinity in Process* (Minneapolis: Fortress Press, 2008).

terms of creaturely characteristics such as creativity and love.

While process theologians maintain this tension between the God that we know and the God who is always beyond our experience and imagination, process theology, nevertheless, confidently describes God primarily in terms of dynamic and loving relatedness. God is the ultimate relational being – God shapes every experience, providing each moment's experience with a wealth of possibilities, and luring each moment toward wholeness and beauty. God also intimately receives every experience and is shaped by the character of the evolving universe. As theologians David Griffin and John Cobb note, God is the ultimate example of creative-responsive love that we yearn to experience in our most intimate relationships.[17] The ever-changing God is also ever-faithful. Taking seriously the affirmation that "God is love," emerging process theology reclaims well-seasoned theological concepts in unexpected and lively ways. The God who loves us truly moves in and through all things and is moved by each and every creature.

The Adventures of the All-Emerging, Ever-Changing, Fully-Loving God. Traditionally, the words omnipresence, omniscience, and omnipotence have been used to describe God's relationship with the world. Although these terms reflect the influence of the Greek philosophical tradition rather then the Hebraic biblical tradition, they express God's infinity and uniqueness. While some persons

---

[17] John Cobb and David Griffin, *Process Theology: An Introductory Exposition* (Louisville: Westminster/John Knox, 1976), 41-62.

believe traditional theological terms must be jettisoned because of their identification with God as unchanging and all-powerful, I believe that in reclaiming the *omni-words* in new ways, emerging process theology describes God's nature, experience, and power in ways that preserve the deepest insights of the Christian theological tradition, yet push beyond the tradition toward novel understandings of the God whose vision energizes, inspires, nurtures, and propels forward human life and its emerging environment. Process theology invites Christians to re-imagine words like "eternal" and "unchanging" in creative ways as descriptions of a Living God who is intimate, loving, responsive, and faithful beyond our wildest imaginings.

The theological term *omniscience* (all-experiencing or all-knowing) relates to the nature and scope of God's experience of the world. Process theology takes the doctrine of divine omniscience seriously as expressing God's dynamic relationship with the emerging universe. God truly experiences the world, that is, God experiences the world directly and intimately in real time as each and every moment of experience unfolds.

Emerging process theology notes the obvious, though neglected aspect of divine experience: to experience anything, whether a creature or the universe as a whole, is to be shaped by what we experience. As omniscient, God is shaped, or conditioned, by all things. Accordingly, everything truly makes a difference to God. Further, if the universe is dynamic and ever-changing, then God's own experience must also be constantly changing and evolving.

The image of a God who truly and fully experiences the universe and our lives changes the way we look at traditional Christian practices. For example, when we pray, our prayers truly make a difference to God and bring something new into God's experience. While God intimately experiences our prayer life, the fact that we pray – and there is no *one* ideal type of prayer – creates new possibilities for God's activity in the world that would not have occurred apart from our prayers. God weaves our prayers with the events of the world in order to bring about the best possibilities for those for whom we pray as well as the broader universe. Without the impact of our prayers and good thoughts, God could not fully exercise God's vision for our world. Our prayers create a field of resonance, a positive environment around those for persons or situations about whom we pray that opens the door to greater revelations of God's presence and power.

In describing the evolving character of divine knowledge, process theology asserts that God's knowledge does not create the future in its actuality, nor does God know the future as actual in advance. God knows future possibilities as possible, and past and present actualities as actual. God does not micromanage, but carefully and artistically brings about the best possibilities in every situation. God is not imprisoned by a timeless and unchanging awareness of the world, but freely moves through our lives inspiring each moment's decision and responding to each moment's emerging uniqueness. God is the God of the living present and the emerging future, freely using the past as the stepping stone to new possibilities.

God's knowledge is all-embracing, ever-expanding, and everlasting; accordingly, everything we do is treasured by God. From this perspective, we truly make a difference to God. Our ethical actions and spiritual commitments truly "do something beautiful for God," to use the language of Mother Teresa of Calcutta.

God's experience of the world is constantly changing and growing, in such a way that our lives truly are our gifts to God. In a world of constant change, still there are certain constants in the divine nature: God's love, aim at beauty, and completeness of experience are both unchanging and unsurpassable. God experiences our lives and the world as it is, objectively; but God also experiences the world with a bias and perspective, the divine desire for loving transformation of even the most horrific and destructive experiences. God sees the world through eyes of love, and is truly touched by our emotions and efforts.

Often theologians have glorified changelessness and eternity as the highest religious values and characteristics of the divine. In contrast, process theology asserts that a changing God, who can occasionally be "surprised" by the world, is the truly living God, the holy companion who initiates new possibilities so that the ever-changing world moment by moment and over the long-haul might more fully reflect God's vision of Shalom.

While some theological viewpoints that identify divine perfection with changeless awareness by which God knows the universe in its entirety prior to the emergence of creation, process theology affirms that a God to whom new things happen is more alive and worshipful than an unchanging, unmoving God. The Calvinistic image of a God who foreknows and predestines all things is the God of boredom and death, not the God of creativity and life. Such a God is limited by God's own eternal decisions and can do nothing new; everyday is like the movie "Groundhog Day" in which God experiences the same things over and over again.

As I stated earlier, emerging process theology affirms that in the unfolding of our lives and the universe, our experiences and prayers shape the quality of God's experience. We matter to the Living God, who has inscribed our lives "on the palm of God's hand" and who "numbers the hairs on our head." Fully in touch with our lives, God is "the fellow sufferer who understands" and the fellow celebrant who rejoices.

The grand theological word *omnipresence* (all-present, everywhere present) suggests that wherever we are, God is present. This is the wisdom of Psalm 139, "if I ascend into the heavens, you are there; if I descend into the depths, you are also there." God is present as the primary influence in each unique moment and in the entire evolutionary process. God's presence is both universal and intimate – we experience God in terms of the constancy of God's ideal for the moment and God's experience of our lives and the universe, even when we are not consciously aware of God. From this perspective, spiritual practices are intended to awaken us to what is ever-present, though constantly variable, in our experience – the Living God in whom all things "live and move and have their being." (Acts 17:28) There are no unimportant or god-forsaken parts of the universe. When we see omnipresence and omniscience in relational terms, then we can affirm "God in all things, and all things in God."

Any discussion of God's presence in the universe leads to the question of God's power, typically understood in terms of *omnipotence* (all-powerful or ultimate power). As a process theologian, I prefer the word *omni-activity* to describe the character of God's power in the world, due to the conflicting images and coercive implications of the word "omnipotence."

To exist is to make a difference, and this applies to cats, dogs, molecules, planets, and persons, as well as God, who lives and moves in all things. However, when we ask the question of the nature of divine activity, we need to consider questions such as: What difference does God's existence make in our lives and in the world? Think for a moment, how do you view God's activity in your life and the world? Does God plan and accomplish everything, from terrorist actions to cancer and heart disease and winning the lottery and being born in a healthy family, or is there an element of freedom or chance in our lives and the universe? Did God cause the earthquake in Haiti in response to the peoples' earlier "pact with the devil," as televangelist Pat Robertson suggested? Does God encourage creativity or treasure the status quo?

Often the words "God's will" are used to describe God's power in the world. According to some theologians, God's power is all-determining: either by divine action or divine permission, God causes or enables everything to occur. God is, accordingly, the source of both good and evil and, if we follow extreme forms of Calvinist theology, salvation and damnation. Other Christian teachers, such as Rick Warren, affirm that God plans all the details of our lives without our input. God's relationship to the world is, from this perspective, linear and unilateral. God creates, but does not receive. God speaks, but does not listen. Passive obedience rather than lively creativity reflects the appropriate response to an all-determining unilateral God.

In contrast, process thought sees divine power as relational rather than coercive. God works within the ecology of life to bring about the best possibilities. Like a good parent, God sets the stage for new forms of freedom and creativity.

Good parenting leaves space for growth: in like fashion, God's "parenting" leaves room for creaturely freedom. God invites us to "color outside the lines" as we bring new things into the universe. In an emerging, adventurous universe, an equally creative and adventurous God is more concerned with our love and creativity than our obedience to particular rules or standards. God does not demand, but inspires. God does not coerce, but liberates our imaginations, even our imaginative images about God. Like a loving parent, God says to God's children, "surprise me – create something new, make something that even I haven't fully thought about yet!"

Emerging process theology asserts that God does not determine all things. Rather, God works gently in the evolutionary process to bring about more complex creatures, capable of experiencing greater and more intense forms of beauty and creativity. Relationships in a process universe are never unilateral, but many-faceted and interdependent. God is *one* of the factors, but not the only factor, in the emergent creativity of each moment of experience. God's power is best described in terms of an inspiring and loving companionship, and not sovereign determinism. Our input truly matters to God. By aligning ourselves with God's vision for our lives, we open new possibilities for divine action. By turning away from God, we limit what God can do in our lives. Pain and suffering emerge from the dynamic interdependence of creaturely decisions, both human and non-human. The future is open for us and for God alike, and while there are no guarantees of success, we can trust God that will creatively respond to every situation, past, present, and future, seeking the highest possibilities for each and every creature.

To summarize, emerging process theology makes the following affirmations about God's relationship and activity in the world:

- *God is present lovingly in every moment of life.*
- *God seeks beauty, complexity, and wholeness in each moment of life.*
- *God truly experiences the world and is shaped by the world that God experiences.*
- *Divine power is relational, and not coercive.*
- *Each moment arises from many factors, the most significant of which is God's presence in that moment.*

· *God supports our creativity and freedom in ways that our congruent with the well-being of our immediate environment and the planet as a whole.*
· *God enters our lives in many ways, responding in the ways that bring wholeness to each moment of our lives.*

Living Process
An Emerging Spiritual Practice

Process theology believes that God is experienced in the still, small voice of love and possibility within the many voices of experience. In fact, process theology affirms that God has many voices and visions for each moment in the dynamic of call and response. In this exercise, close your eyes and simply listen. What voices do you hear in the silence? What pushes and pulls are there in the silence? Now, listen more deeply – Do you hear a voice of loving possibility, of abundant life? Do you hear a call toward responsible freedom and creativity? Do you experience a call toward a healthy future for yourself, others, and the planet?

In the spirit of divine omnipresence, this second exercise involves "praying with your senses" or "praying with your eyes open." Begin by taking a few minutes to quietly breathe in the spirit of God. As you continue gently breathing, simply notice the wonder of each moment...notice the wonder of taste...the holiness of sight...the harmony of hearing...the aroma of smelling...the gentle caress of touch. Pause and notice God entering your experience with every sensation. Experience the wonder and glory of the universe and the God who moves through each and every thing. In conclusion, take time to give thanks as you experience the profound interdependence of life and your relationship with God.

Throughout the day, whenever you notice your breath, repeat the affirmation, "God inspires and energizes me with every breath."

Chapter Three

Revealing God: Truth and Pluralism

Then Paul stood in front of the Areopagus and said, "Athenians, I see how extremely religious you are in every way. For as I went through the city and looked carefully at the objects of your worship, I found among them an altar with the inscription, 'To an unknown God.' What therefore you worship as unknown, this I proclaim to you. The God who made the world and everything in it, the one who is the God of heaven, does not live in shrines made by human hands....indeed this God is not far from each one of us. For, 'In God we live and move and have our being'; as even some of your own poets have said, 'For we too are God's offspring.'" [18]

PAUL'S WORDS TO THE ATHENIAN intellectual community set the stage for a postmodern, emerging process understanding of truth, revelation, and pluralism.

---

[18] Acts 17:24, 28

Postmodern thought challenges any uniform and global understanding of reality. Postmodern thinkers see truth as relational, experiential, and communal in nature. Revelation is given not to persons in the abstract, but right here and now to lively, concrete, and fallible persons and communities. Truth and wisdom are evolving and emerging in an "open source" network arising from the interactions of many voices and religious and cultural perspectives. Further, the receiver contributes her experience to whatever revelation she receives, whether mystical or inspired by scripture, sermon, or sunset.

Paul's message at the Athenian Areopagus reflects the polyvalent nature of truth-seeking and truth-speaking in our pluralistic, postmodern age. Although Paul's words to the intellectual community were definitely confessional and evangelistic in style, his approach was also appreciative and contextual. Before he said a word about the transforming power of Jesus Christ, he got to know the beliefs and lifestyle of those with whom he spoke. He even invoked the wisdom of Greek philosophy as illuminating his own vision of God. Paul proclaimed his vision of Christ in terms of the "unknown" yet sought after source of wholeness in the context of his affirmation of the cultural and religious pluralism of Athens.

Paul's sermon at the Areopagus was a far cry from the approach of an "open air" evangelist who daily preached on a hillside in front of the Humanities Building at Central Michigan University where I taught in the early 1980's. Shouting scripture passages and threats of eternal damnation at students, staff, and faculty passing by, this evangelist may have thought he was imitating Paul's message at the Areopagus; but, there was one big difference, he spoke but did not listen. He did not bother to learn about the passersby's hopes or struggles or even their faith commitments. He assumed that all his listeners were lost, even if they were practicing Christians, and that his listeners could find their way to God only by accepting his message. For him, there was no point of contact between the doctrines he preached and the experiences of the passersby or the content of courses taught in the Humanities building. From his, and from most conservative religious perspectives, truth and salvation are limited, narrowly confined to an easily memorized and absolutely clear list of doctrinal statements; outside the "church" – and this can be Christianity as a whole or a small house church - there is no salvation! Closed system truths exclude everyone except those who recite the right words and follow the right biblical interpretations. Perhaps, this open air evangelist thought the shouted word alone in all its vehemence and condemnation, without any relationship to the living human beings walking by, could transform and heal persons' lives.

One day, on my way to class, I decided to pause right in the front of the speaker. I hoped to engage him in conversation and learn about his journey of faith. Sadly, he continued his harangue as if he did not even notice I was there. I realized that he, like so many others, who condemn spiritual seekers, gay, lesbian, and transgendered persons, and persons of other faiths, see "others" in terms of abstractions and caricatures, and not their flesh and blood daily experiences of love, celebration, fear, and doubt. He could glibly condemn unbelievers to hell precisely because they had no flesh and blood existence apart from being objects of his proselytizing. Sadly, his message was as abstract and irrelevant to their lived experience as was his theology.

As they ponder the nature of truth and revelation, many postmodern thinkers assert that our communal and personal narratives are entirely personal and perspectival in nature, and have no validity beyond the confines of our particular tribe or community experience. Other postmodern thinkers note that while there are no global stories or universal truths, applicable to all times and places, there are life-transforming regional and local stories, inspirational within the context of particular theological, spiritual, or cultural tribes or communities. From this perspective, often described as constructive postmodernism, the theological quest involves listening to the experiences and world views of other communities in the context of sharing our own life-changing stories of God, faith, and wholeness. In the process, our own stories grow in breadth, depth, and insight, and we may discover a common theological and spiritual ground that joins our many stories. In this open source network of inspiration, we grow, like young Jesus, in "wisdom and stature" as persons of faith, who by our contributions to our own faith traditions enable these traditions also to become more inclusive and insightful in describing the world in which we live. (Luke 2:52)

As a form of constructive postmodern thinking, process theology dares to tell a large story, the story of an evolving cosmos and the movements of a lively, relational, and creative God. Although always known and described from many varied and particular vantage points, this large story embraces the myriad evolving and contrasting communal stories and narratives of faith. Truth and revelation, like reality itself, are relational, dynamic, shape-shifting, and ever-growing. While some may critique the many-faceted quest for truth characteristic of postmodern thought and process theology, process theologians affirm that while all people experience God's universal presence in the depths of their being, each one of us also experiences God from her or his vantage point. Each of our experiences of God is shaped by our personal, family, communal, generational, scientific, and religious perspective. No two stories are entirely alike, because no two persons are entirely alike in DNA, life experience, family of origin, and responsiveness to the world. Indeed, each of us encounters a "different God" insofar as the God who moves through all creatures intimately reaches out to each creature. This is the practical meaning of omnipresence: God is lovingly present, enlivening and inspiring me, even when I am unaware of it, in every moment of experience.

Just think of it: no one experiences the universe from your perspective; no two moments of your own experience are repeatable; each moment is a lively, creative synthesis of the universe, including God; your next moment of experience will embrace the past, yet bring a new perspective, indeed, a new truth, to the universe. What an adventurous world we live in! What an adventurous life you have! Rather than devaluating our personal experiences, emerging process theology affirms their unique ability to reveal the Living God. The protean and multi-faceted God is a different God for each one of us: though universal in impact and revelation, God is also intimately seeking the wholeness that we need, and revealing what we need to find meaning, within our time and place.

The Hindu tradition describes the many-faceted nature of truth and revelation in terms of a group of sight-impaired persons, each of whom is attempting to portray the "true" nature of an elephant. To one, the reality of the elephant is its trunk; to another, its legs; to a third, its tusk; and to a fourth, its tail. Each of the persons is correct from her or his perspective, but none of them fully encompasses the reality that he or she attempts to describe. Emerging process theology goes one step further. A living, breathing elephant itself is in process. Sometimes the elephant is running; other times, it's chewing; still other times, the elephant is calling to its companions. Those who attempt to describe the elephant must hang on for dear life and may, over time, discover not only the tail, but also the trunk, ears, tusk, and legs! Like the legendary elephant, God, as envisaged by emerging process theology, is never stable or fixed in one place, but always in process, constantly moving and always much more than we describe. Faithfulness to the moving and evolving God involves openness to truth in its many and diverse, even contrasting and ever-changing, media. It involves having the agility of faith to embrace new perspectives as we encounter new dimensions of the divine-human call and response.

The quest for truth in a pluralistic age is always a creative process in which we are receivers, artists, and designers of the evolving truths we hold dearly. For many of us, and for many of today's seekers, the spiritual quest has taken us down many pathways. Nearly forty years ago, I encountered Gilbert, a long-haired "Jesus freak," a sixties term for hippie-types who claimed Jesus as their personal savior. When I first met Gilbert, every other sentence contained the words "praise the Lord" as he regularly testified to how "Jesus had saved him from a life of drugs, sex, and rock and roll." After the Christmas break, when I next encountered Gilbert, his hair was shaved and he was wearing the robe of a Hare Krishna, an incarnation of the Hindu God Vishnu. He confessed that in chanting the name of Krishna, he found spiritual practice that gave him true joy. A year later, we were both part of Transcendental Meditation group, meeting on campus. When I last heard from Gilbert, he was practicing Buddhist meditation along with Hindu Yoga and astrology. Sometimes I wonder what adventures of the spirit Gilbert has taken since college. I hope he is still growing in his understanding of the divine, and that he has found a way to holistically and creatively embrace and synthesize the many pathways he has traveled.

To some degree, we are always creating our faith as we go along. Some people denounce this dynamic quest to experience the Holy as "designer religion," a narcissistic turn from the clearly articulated and objective "old time religion" of our parents in the faith to purely individualistic and relativistic spirituality. But, from the perspective of emerging process theology, commitment to the way of Jesus constantly challenges us to create and re-create our faith stories, since our lives and experiences evolve in light of new experiences of God, the world, and our most immediate communities. In the spirit of the ever-fluid, ever-creative, Proteus, our personal faith changes shape as we grow and as we commit ourselves to dialogue with past, present, and future spiritual communities. This was surely true of the earliest Christians, whose spiritual quests took them beyond Judaism and its rituals and rules. As they transformed the world by their encounter with Jesus, they also found themselves transformed in their encounters with Greek philosophy, the Greek language of the New Testament, and the spiritual traditions of Egypt, Asia Minor, Europe, the British Isles, and Arabia. In many ways, these early followers of Jesus, as described in Acts of the Apostles, were also making it up as they went along, trying to make sense of their mystical experiences, miraculous moments, and ever-enlarging community of faith, in light of the stories of Jesus, the wisdom of Greek philosophy, and the Hebraic tradition in which many of them were raised.

As I look at my own faith journey, I chart my quest for truth and wholeness in terms of widening circles of inspiration and embodiment: emerging from evangelical Baptist roots to embrace the psychedelic experiences of the "summer of love," the practice of Transcendental Meditation, Platonic philosophy and its quest for the eternal in the midst of ever-flowing time, the social gospel and political activism, Christian meditation and mysticism, complementary medicine and the healings of Jesus, and progressive, spirit-centered process theology, lived out in my life as a professor, pastor, and spiritual guide. Strongly rooted in the way of Jesus, I believe that faithful integrity still means making it up as I go along in encounters with the insights of physicists, cosmologists, spiritual healers, atheists and agnostics, persons of other faiths, and Christians of many perspectives. My experience mirrors not only my generation's protean faith stories, but also the spiritual vision of emerging Christianity and its inclusion of ancient, present, and future images of faith, worship, and spiritual practice. Now, in my late fifties, I look forward with anticipation to experiencing new facets of the divine as I face what lies ahead in my own holy adventure in companionship with God: my own aging, the joy of being a grandparent, the realities of global climate change and the death of the American Empire, new perspectives on the universe, new spiritual practices, and new ways to live out my profession as a teacher, healer, and spiritual guide. I believe that wherever there is life, there is creativity, growth, and transformation. Deeply rooted in the way of Jesus, I too am daily designing a life of faith as I join seamlessly the spiritual disciplines of reiki healing touch, contemplative and intercessory prayer, biblical affirmations, and the transcendental meditation I first learned in 1970.

My own spiritual eclecticism reflects the polyvalent personal revelations of a protean and personal God. In receiving and sharing revelation, my faith is rooted in an Open Source who generously gives revelation through every encounter and tradition.

Emerging process theology affirms that the lively, open-spirited, and ever-changing God is present in the birth of every moment of experience. Deep down, each moment arises from God's intimately directed vision and energy that sets its creative adventure in motion. God blesses each emerging moment with an inner desire to become something novel and beautiful both for itself and for the wider universe. While we often turn away from God's vision, burying it deeply in our unconscious mind, God will continue to "stand at the door and knock," presenting us with a vision appropriate to our current experience, life-situation, and global context.

Divine revelation is global, touching and energizing all things; but it is also intensely personal, inspiring *each* thing. Different experiences of the divine are not accidental, nor are they a fall from grace. Rather, they reflect the evolving call of an infinitely creative and personal God and the response of a myriad of creatures each in its cultural context.

In contrast to an open source approach to revelation, certain Christians assert that there is only *one* truth and *one* way to experience salvation. They assert that if we miss that one truth or one way, we are doomed to meaninglessness in this life and condemnation in the next. Knowing only one way of salvation, these followers assume that the God they worship demands obedience and subservience as essential religious virtues. Their God creates a tightly circumscribed closed system in which outsiders outnumber insiders and truth is unchanging and exclusionary.

Emerging process theology takes another path in its affirmation of many visions of God, embodied by the evolving world religions as well as our more personal faith journeys, each of which reflects God's call to a person or community. Revelation is both universal and variable. Simply put, while God loves and inspires every creature, God can choose certain creatures and certain moments to become uniquely representative of God's vision for a particular cultural and faith community. These revelations, however, are not different in kind from other creatures' experiences of the divine; rather, they differ in terms of divine-human intentionality and call and response. Process thought can affirm that the God of all creation chose Jesus to be a world-transforming revelation of God's vision, rooted in the wisdom, creativity, inspiration, and current historical situation of the Hebraic people. This was not an eternal or timeless choice, contemplated before the creation of the world, but the result of the movements of creative wisdom in a particular time and place and in response to a particular person, family, historical tradition, and faith community. Still, Jesus had to say "yes" to the ongoing call of the spirit and, then, throughout his life, constantly open himself to God's vision for him as a teacher, healer, prophet, and faith-transformer. Jesus' "yes" in life and death still shapes our lives, awakening us to divine wisdom and healing power.

Jesus' personal quest for alignment with God's vision for his life and the world was hard work: as scripture notes, he was tempted and tried like ourselves, but knew no sin, that is, Jesus saw himself wholly and

71

fully before God, whether his experiences involved temptation in the wilderness or the desire for survival in the Garden of Gethsemene. Even on the Cross, Jesus' agony did not diminish his sense of God's presence. Abandoned by his followers and tormented by his foes, Jesus still chose to be an instrument of grace as he proclaimed, "Father, forgive them, for they know not what they do."

Emerging process theologians affirm that the God who empowered, energized, and enlightened Jesus was also present in Jesus' prophetic predecessors as well as in the life and teachings of his distant followers, the prophet Mohammed and the founders of the Bahai faith. God's inspiration energized and guided Gautama as he sought enlightenment under the Bo tree and inspired Lao Tzu's vision of simplicity and awareness. In each of these revelatory persons, and also in our own experiences today, God reveals something unique and inspirational for the transformation of the world.

Whitehead notes that the world lives by the incarnation of God.[19] Personally speaking, this means that we too live by the incarnation of God and can gratefully affirm: "I live by the incarnation of God and you live by the incarnation of God." Those who call themselves followers of Jesus most especially center their lives and experiences around God's wisdom as revealed in the life of Jesus and the evolving Christian story in all its diversity, wonder, and imperfection. As followers of Jesus, our response to God's presence in our lives brings

---

[19] Whitehead, *Religion in the Making,* 149.

us closer or further from our personal and communal vocation in this moment and over a lifetime. With the German mystic Meister Eckhart, we can affirm that all things are words of God even as we proclaim the uniqueness of the Embodied Word in the life, healings, and teachings of Jesus of Nazareth. There is enough truth to go around in the many paths of faith. In an open-system universe, truth is not a scarce commodity, a "zero-sum" game, or a finished product, but a constantly evolving kaleidoscope of images and experiences that transform persons and cultures. We can affirm wholeheartedly the significance of Jesus in our personal transformation and the faith of our community, while recognizing and embracing the wisdom and practices of other faith traditions.

Here, however, emerging process must respond to those for whom traditional understandings of Christianity of the creeds and scripture are definitive and unwavering. Does the many-faceted nature of revelation mean that there are no truths that are global and that we are condemned to hopeless relativism, in which all we can do is affirm our own perspective and accept the sometimes violent and destructive perspectives of others? Does emerging process thought possess an unswerving point of view from which to evaluate other religious pathways, including other paths within Christianity?

Emerging process theology presents a life-changing vision of the divine and human adventures, but recognizes the limitation of all pathways toward wholeness, including process theology itself. Once again, the dynamic interdependence of the *apophatic* and *kataphatic*

73

approaches to truth and revelation provides a pathway to humble affirmation of the truths we experience. Process thought recognizes the treasures revealed in our encounters with God, recognizing their transformative power. But, emerging process theology also recognizes, with the Apostle Paul that we have these life-transforming and healing treasures in earthen vessels. We see truth enough to transform our lives: we glimpse the movements of God in our lives and faith communities, but we see in a mirror dimly even as we await fully revelations of divine wisdom.

Our spiritual and theological self-affirmations cannot escape the protean and lively Holy Adventure that gives them birth. The lively and constantly evolving God is always beyond our understanding, even when God is most present within our experience. We can't encompass God, nor will God stand still or be imprisoned and objectified by a particular book or ritual. Still, the universality of revelation gives us confidence that our highest inclinations, noblest aspirations, and greatest dreams constantly emerge from the dance of divine call and human response, and human call and divine response. The God who is always "more" is also always "here," inviting and enlightening us at some deep level and, on occasion, transforming our whole way of experiencing reality. God touches us in many ways and through many names.

With Brian McLaren, we must be generous in our orthodoxy, noting that God can reveal Godself through Pentecostal tongue speaking, Benedictine silence, evangelical passion, liberal social action, and progressive inclusiveness, but more than that, the free and unbounded spirit blows through ancient faiths in Africa and North and South America as well as ashrams in India. God's voice can be heard through an imam's call to prayer or a Zen Buddhist koan. Bountiful in revelation, the God, described by emerging process, also speaks in the careful voice of the skeptic and the challenge of the atheist and her vision of a god she cannot believe in.

While we cannot absolutize our vision of truth, we can experience truths that save and transform in our growing understanding of our own faith as well as the ongoing dialogue with other faith traditions and the insights of literature, psychology, science, and culture. As Christians, we find truths to live by in Jesus' vision of an all-embracing loving God, who welcomes outcasts, searches for the lost, heals the broken, and embraces the foreigner. Our good news as Christians in an age of pluralism is that God wants us to have abundant life and that God also wants everyone else to have abundant life in all its many forms. Living this good news is the heart of our mission.

We cannot describe truth in its fullness; but we can proclaim truths and insights, revelations, that are "good enough" and "broad enough" to enable us to live courageously and sacrificially, to pursue justice and planetary survival, and face chronic illness, debilitation, aging, and death with hope in God's everlasting love and vision for all things.

Good Enough Scripture. I must confess that I am a biblical Christian. I preach most Sundays of the month, write lectionary commentaries for Process and Faith and

Patheos on a regular basis, and consult scripture as a source of affirmations and guidance.[20]   This close relationship to the bible began in the Baptist household and congregation of my childhood. Each morning we had biblical devotions at home and at Sunday school, we often sang:

> *The B-I-B-L-E, oh that's the book for me,*
> *I stand alone on the word of God,*
> *the B-I-B-L-E.*

Although I am grateful for the "bible drills" of my childhood and can still race through the scriptures to find the passage I'm looking for, today, like many other Christians, I feel a good deal of ambivalence about the way scripture is often used to exclude, oppress, or silence those whose beliefs and life experiences fall outside literal interpretations of the scripture.

Recently my wife Kate was told she would burn in hell because, as a member of Silent Witness, a group committed to providing peaceful support of persons attending Gay Pride events, she is open and affirming of gay, lesbian, transgendered, bi-sexual, and questioning persons. Her accuser based his condemnation on a handful of opaque scriptural passages, none of which relate to loving and supportive homosexual relationships. Similar passages have been used in the past to condemn divorce and bar divorced persons from ministry, justify

---

[20] www.processandfaith.org and www.patheos.com

slavery, deny women's rights and the ordination of women into Christian ministry, and compel persons to remain in abusive marriages. If this were all we knew of scripture, we would have to reject it as bad news for ourselves and persons at the fringes of society. More than once, I have surprised non-Christian seekers when I shared our congregation's hospitality all persons, including LGBT persons, our openness to other faiths and practice of reiki healing touch, and our belief in universal salvation and saving revelation. Assuming that all Christians are biblical literalists, they have difficulty imagining that a person could be both Christian and progressive or a follower of Jesus and affirm other faith traditions!

Postmodern thinkers constantly remind us that all authority and revelation, and all claims to truth are local and perspectival; this understanding of authority must even include the sacred scriptures of our own and other religious traditions. Spiritual authority, experienced or written, is grounded in its ability to transform persons' lives and illuminate our experiences of joy and sorrow, and not some unquestioned foundation or interpretive principle. Recently I heard a sermon describing "infallible proofs for the resurrection." While I sympathized with the preacher's quest for certainty, I was amazed at his logic: we can infallibly prove the resurrection simply because it is testified to in a number of New Testament passages, which are assumed to be factually accurate because they are in the Bible. Such circular reasoning, however, demands a theological foundation which can be asserted only within a closed system of believers, but not proven or universally experienced or accepted by persons outside the circle of biblical literalism. Put simply, scripture is infallible or inerrant because it says – or our church says – that it is infallible and inerrant.

Emerging process theologians recognize the inspirational power of the Bible to transform communities. But, in light of our understanding of truth and pluralism, how shall we understand the nature of biblical revelation? Can we find comfort and inspiration in a text that reveals both the insights and fallibilities, and the universality and particularity that characterize all revelatory experiences? Can we have a "good enough" bible for the twenty-first century? Put, another way, can we have revelation that is "good enough" even if it is limited and fallible? Perhaps just as important, can we reclaim the Bible from biblical literalists?

Once again, emerging process theology avoids the contrasting pitfalls of literalism and relativism. While some Christians glibly proclaim "the Bible says it, I believe it, and that settles it," emerging process theology recognizes that scripture's ability to inspire, guide, and transform people's lives arises from its concreteness, intimacy, and historical context. Reading scripture changes lives precisely because it is a personal and historical word. A universal, timeless, and absolute scripture can neither encourage nor transform us. Emerging process theology recognizes that scripture itself is uneven; some passages reflect the highest visions of humankind, while others endorse the basest human emotions and behaviors – violence against women, destruction of innocent peoples, displacement of native peoples, and the hatred of opponents. In order to be faithful to the lively God who inspired the communities that gave words to God's wisdom, we have no alternative but to challenge violent and hate-filled scriptural passages as unworthy of the God of Jesus Christ.

Still, we are forced to ask: In what way, however, is scripture inspired? And, is its inspiration different in kind than other holy books, theological texts, or literature? Why do we take scripture more seriously than a current best seller in spiritual self-help or new age literature "channeled" by a spiritual being? On what basis should we "pick and choose" certain passages as important to our faith?

In the context of its understanding of revelation as universal, process theology cannot give the bible unique, sole, and absolute privilege in terms of inspiration. God is present in every quest for truth and healing, and every decisive spiritual moment in the lives of persons and communities. While the bible uniquely describes the spiritual and communal adventures of the Hebrews and Christians, other faiths can also claim unique inspiration in their own spiritual texts. Accordingly, while claiming the centrality of scripture in our understanding of God as Christians, we can see other sacred texts as complementing the wisdom and insight we find in the bible. When we read other spiritual texts, for example the Tao Te Ching, Upanishads, Qur'an, or Buddhist Diamond Sutra, alongside our own scriptures, our own faith grows in depth and insight. The wisdom found in contemporary spiritual, theological, and literary texts also reflects God's inspiration in ways that can transform our lives.

Think for a moment of your own spiritual journey: What texts have deepened your insights into the nature of human life and the world in which we live? Were all of them written by "Christian" writers? Would you describe these texts as "inspired" by God? Are some of your insights also "inspired" by God in ways that illuminate others as well as your own journey?

As I chart my own spiritual journey, I experienced transformation reading the meditative texts of Vietnamese Buddhist Thich Naht Hanh, the writings of process theologians, the fictional narratives of Madeleine L'Engle, the autobiographical journeys of Anne Lamott and Frederick Buechner, and the relational and congregational systems wisdom of Edwin Friedman, along with hundreds of other Christian and non-Christian texts. Surely God was present in the writing and reading of these books, speaking a word of graceful transformation that shaped my personal and professional life.

Emerging process theology understands scripture not as one book, unified in theology and viewpoint, but as a variety of texts, indeed, a living library of texts, reflecting the interplay of persons and communities with the divine. God inspired the writing and collection of scripture, but more fundamentally, God inspired the lives, persons, and communal process that brought forth the books of the bible. Like any written text, including this text, scripture describes only the tip of the iceberg in terms of fullness and power of divine inspiration and human experience of God and not the whole picture. Accordingly, emerging process theology sees wisdom in the recently discovered Gospel of Thomas and other nonbiblical portraits of Jesus and his teachings. The dynamic reality of God is always more than the words of scripture and the experiences of the communities that brought it forth.

As a library of texts, we have to assume a variability of biblical divine inspiration and human response. Even fundamentalists hold that some texts are more important than others in the life of faith. Biblical literalists assume that the cleanliness codes of the Hebraic community are no longer in force as they enjoy their Easter ham dinners. Nevertheless, they maintain the significance equally ancient and irrelevant Hebraic prohibitions of homosexuality and divorce and assume God's hand was behind the destruction of Sodom and Gemmorah.

The variability of revelation and evolving importance in our spiritual adventures is found in the dynamic process of call and response present in scripture itself. For example, Job challenges understandings of good fortune and suffering that assume that persons' prosperity is a reflection of their piety and morality, while persons' poverty and illness reflects behaviors worthy of divine punishment. Jonah's universalistic message of God's love challenges parochial and vindictive visions of election and nationalism held by many of his fellow citizens and enshrined in popular religion. Jesus' "but, I say unto you" sayings from the Sermon on the Mount reflect his understanding of the deeper meaning of the Hebraic scriptures. God is constantly speaking, revelation is always evolving; new situations call for new responses and understandings of God.

In conclusion, emerging process theologians see scripture as a window into the ongoing dynamic process of divine and human call and response, or divine-human conversation. Our scriptures portray pivotal moments in which persons experienced God's presence in life-transforming ways that not only shaped their lives but the lives of their communities. These words shape our lives and communities today. Accordingly, emerging process theology proclaims that, from the standpoint of divine call and creaturely response, the canon of inspiration is still open. Biblical inspiration calls persons today to recognize where God has spoken in the past and awaken to emerging divine inspiration in the present and the future. God is revealed in the most insightful sayings of the Desert Fathers, Celtic spiritual guides, mystics such as Hildegard and Mechtild; modern voices such as those of Mother Teresa, Martin Luther King, Desmond Tutu, and Billy Graham. God's whisper is found in the writings of process thinkers such as Alfred North Whitehead and Teilhard de Chardin. Nearly forty years ago, I experienced a transformed Christianity in reading the words of Alfred North Whitehead, John Cobb, and Charles Hartshorne. While these voices do not carry the traditional authority of scripture in the life of the church, they do have the power to transform and energize persons and communities. Still, emerging process reminds us that we also continue to hear God's voice in other tongues, in First American prayers, the proclamations of Mohammed, the gentle counsel of Lao Tzu and the everyday wisdom of Confucius as well as in the spiritual counsel of the Dalai Lama. All these voices can be heard alongside the teachings of Jesus and the Hebraic prophets in Christian worship and spiritual care. God is still speaking. Revelation evolves and emerges. And we too can be voices of God sharing in and contributing to God's ongoing inspiration.

Living Process
An Emerging Spiritual Practice

In this exercise, take a moment to "listen to your life." Remember a moment when God was truly real to you. Go back in your memory to visualize that moment. Experience God's nearness and inspiration in that moment. Rejoice in its unique revelation of the divine. Now, looking at your life today, what guidance does that moment give you as you consider your current life situation? What actions and commitments does this experience inspire you to today?

In the following exercise, imaginatively reflect on your relationship to scripture. What scriptures or books have been most significant in your spiritual journey? When has a particular scripture or text inspired or comforted you? Take time to remember that experience and the impact it had on your life. In contrast, reflect on those scriptures or books that you have found problematic? Why are they problematic? Why might they be harmful to your faith or to the faith of another?

Chapter Four

Jesus the Healer

I have come that they may have life, and have it abundantly.[21]

IN OCTOBER 2007, OUR ONLY SON MATT was diagnosed with a rare and life-threatening form of cancer that turned our parental world upside down. During his treatment and the subsequent months that followed, hundreds of people prayed for him, he received reiki treatments, repeated affirmations, and meditated on a daily basis. He received regular hands-on healing treatments from a Christian energy worker, known for her "hot hands" and acupuncture treatments from a holistic psychiatrist. But, he also received chemotherapy and took medication to reduce the symptoms of his treatment. Today, Matt and his wife are looking toward a long and joyous life ahead, and are rejoicing with a healthy and happy baby. His recovery is the result of the interplay of the modern western medicine, complementary health techniques, and spiritual practices. Our family's response to Matt's diagnosis reflected our belief that God works for healing

---

[21] John 10:10

in all things and that both meditation and medication can transform our lives.

Progressive and process-oriented Christians are often conflicted about Jesus. Many of us are scandalized by Christians who proclaim that Jesus is the *only* way to salvation. We are equally troubled by those who see Jesus as a completely supernatural figure, untouched by the realities of pain, aging, conflict, and human finitude. We rebel against dualistic understandings of Jesus that assert that Jesus was in some way omniscient or omnipotent, or was merely a human body in which a divine microchip was somehow inserted. While many progressive and process-oriented Christians lament the fact Jesus' message of healing, hospitality, and love has been hidden by an overemphasis on doctrinal and sacramental orthodoxy, nevertheless, Jesus of Nazareth, the teacher, healer, and spirit person remains at the heart of their faith.

Many progressive Christians also struggle with supernatural understandings of Jesus as a divine miracle worker, who could at will arbitrarily violate the laws of nature. Still, progressive and process-oriented Christians recognize that a purely naturalistic and this-worldly Enlightenment understanding of Jesus is theologically inadequate and that we must somehow redefine our understanding of the natural world to include non-local causation (action at a distance), paranormal phenomena, and healing energy. Jesus was not a one-dimensional figure and neither are we! In light of recent medical research on the mind-body relationship, the power of the mind to transform the cells of our bodies, and the ability of distant prayers to contribute to the well-being of others, we need to reevaluate the healing ministry of Jesus. A deeper, more spiritual, naturalism in dialogue with recent medical research and the insights of global and complementary medicine makes room for Jesus' healing acts, reflective of the deeper insights of the gospel narratives of Jesus' ministry and God's realm of shalom. Emerging process theology's affirmation of God's lively presence in both the human and non-human worlds enables us to experience the gospel stories in novel and life-transforming ways that allow us to expect more from God and more from ourselves than we previously imagined.[22]

While progressive and mainline Christians recognize the relativity and imperfection of the biblical narratives, including the gospel accounts of Jesus' ministry, process theology affirms that a holistic understanding of Jesus embraces both the gospel portraits of Jesus, including the narratives of resurrection experiences, and the "historical" Jesus who lies behind these narratives. It also takes seriously the non-canonical witness found in other gospel stories, such as *The Gospel of Thomas.* Totally deconstructionist or one-dimensional naturalistic visions of the gospel narratives fail to address the life-transforming experiences of first-century followers of Jesus as well as the profound interdependence of mind, body, and spirit; they also neglect God's activity within

---

[22] See Epperly *God's Touch, Healing Worship: Faith, Wholeness, and the Healing Miracles of Jesus* (Louisville: Westminster/John Knox, 2001) and *Healing Worship: Purpose and Practice* (Cleveland: Pilgrim Press, 2006).

every "natural" process. Indeed, many of the most devastating progressive critiques of Jesus' healing ministry and the resurrection narratives, especially those of John Shelby Spong and John Dominic Crossan, seem to be tied, albeit in a deconstructionist fashion, to Enlightenment metaphysics and reactions to religious conservatism, rather than to the insights of process theology, quantum physics, recent medical research, and global complementary and energy medicine, all of which allow for surprising acts of God and lively releases of divine energy arising from the interplay of "natural" causes.

Today's understandings of Jesus must emerge from what we can faithfully affirm about Jesus' ministry as a teacher and healer rather than focusing on what we must deny in terms of the biblical narratives and the descriptions of Jesus relationship to God (Christology) found in the later Christian tradition.

Process theologians agree with the traditional affirmation that for Jesus to be meaningful and life-transforming for us, we must hold in contrast two polarities of experience: 1) Jesus must be "more" than we are in terms of energy, inspiration, and God-awareness and 2) Jesus must also be like ourselves, completely human and fully like us in nature and experience.

In the quest for a life-transforming Christology, or understanding of the message of Jesus and Jesus' relationship with God, process theology affirms that divine revelation is universal in both scope and impact. God is present as the source of each moment of experience. God provides each moment of experience with possibilities for self-actualization and for its contribution to the self-actualization of others. Since all things are inspired by God, Jesus of Nazareth is not an exception to God's universal aim at beauty and wholeness. Still, a personal and visionary God can also choose to influence creation in various ways and with varied manifestations of energy and intentionality. God is not a homogenous or neutral force; but is dynamically, intimately, and uniquely present in all things. As both personal and transpersonal, God can choose to be more present in some events and moments than others. This was surely the case in God's choice of Jesus as healer and revealer of God's shalom.

Process theologians affirm that God's unique presence in Jesus of Nazareth does not undermine the continuity of Jesus' experience and our own. God chose to be dynamically present in the conception of Mary's child and God chose to be uniquely and energetically present in the life of Jesus. This choice was not foreordained or abstract, but rooted in the ongoing concrete, divine-human call and response in the Hebraic tradition and in the unique spiritual, cultural, and political world of first-century Judaism. Still, Jesus was not a passive recipient of divine power and revelation. While God's grace and power inspired and enlivened Jesus, Jesus' openness to God enabled him to become a clear and powerful mediator of God's realm to the world. This same experience of the God's intimate presence, no doubt, was also true of Mary, the mother of Jesus, whose openness to following God is seen by the scriptures as prerequisite to her bearing God's holy child. (Luke 1:26-38)

89

In the interplay of God's intimate presence and Jesus' receptive and creative response, we find the meaning of the ancient words, "fully human, fully divine." Jesus' full humanity and divinity are spiritually one, and are revealed in his lively manifestation of God's passion for healing and wholeness. Jesus is the ultimate example of the divine-human call and response, toward which we aim in our own ongoing spiritual adventures. As early Christian theologian Iranaeus proclaimed, the glory of God is a fully alive human being. Fully alive, Jesus experienced the fullness of divine possibility, power, and perspective in his concrete historical and limited time and place. Jesus' embodiment of God's vision still transforms persons in our time.

As a fully relational human reflecting the presence of a fully relational God, Jesus experienced the fullness of the world's pain and imperfection as well as its joy and celebration. Yet, his multidimensional and often ambiguous experience of the Roman violence and oppression, Jewish alienation, and the idiosyncrasies of his family of origin, did not lure Jesus away from seeking to experience God's passion in each moment of his life. Jesus was united in the spirit with God, even in his times of growth and temptation. As the Gospel of Luke notes, Jesus grew in "wisdom and stature." (Luke 2:52) Even the highest manifestations of God's presence in the world, revealed in Jesus' spiritual relationship with the Divine Parent, are characterized by continuous intellectual and spiritual growth. As the gospel narrative notes, Jesus' spiritual experience was dynamic and evolving. For example, it appears that Jesus learned something important from a Canaanite woman, who sought comfort for her demon possessed daughter. Her assertive care for her daughter may have challenged Jesus to preach wholeness and salvation to the Gentile world beyond first century Judaism. (Mark7:24-30)

Emerging visions of process theology see the incarnation of God in Christ as the supreme manifestation of God's presence in all things. Process Christology is often described as a "logos theology," following the insights of the first chapter of John's gospel and certain early church fathers. With John's Prologue (John 1:1-5, 9), process theologians see the divine word (*dabhar, sophia, logos*) as the creative and life-giving power in all things. This "true light" shines in all things, not just in human life or Christian experience. As theologian John Cobb affirms, Christ is the principle of "creative transformation," that is, wherever beauty, love, and justice emerge, the power present in Jesus of Nazareth is its source.[23] I would add that "wherever truth and healing are found, Christ is its source, regardless of what names are invoked, Christian or otherwise."

Transforming Atonement. The doctrine of atonement traditionally describes the ways in which Jesus "saves" us, that is, overcomes our brokenness and enables us to experience God's love and passion in our lives. For evangelical Christians, the cross is seen as God's primary vehicle for atonement – "Jesus died for our sins," many

---

[23] John Cobb, *Christ in a Pluralistic Age* (Louisville: Westminster/John Knox, 1975).

evangelicals proclaim. With open-spirited evangelical Christianity, process thinkers affirm that God transforms the world through suffering love, for God is the "fellow sufferer who understands,"[24] but they also assert that Jesus' death was not a sacrifice for our sins, a way to soothe God's anger, or predestined to occur in order to save humanity from its sinfulness. God did not compel Jesus to die, nor does God use his death as a ransom for our sins or the only way to restore God's injured honor. Rather, Jesus transforms us by inspiring us to embody his ideals in our lives, by sharing in our suffering, and by providing pathways for growth in every season of life. In a relational universe, the impact of Jesus' life still influences humankind, empowering, inspiring, and calling us to healing and wholeness. The way of the cross calls us to identify with the suffering of others and to commit ourselves to the healing of the earth and our human and non-human companions. The pathway of resurrection awakens us to God's never ending vision of possibilities, even at the descending edges of life.[25]

Process theology's holistic approach to atonement sees God's saving presence in Jesus in terms of "transformation by touch." The God who is touched by the world, whose presence embodied in Jesus of Nazareth himself is touched by human joy and pain, also touches us in ways that heal, enliven, awaken, and accept. Touched by Jesus, we experience "atonement," that is at-one-ment,

---

[24] Alfred North Whitehead, *Process and Reality,* 351.

[25] For a process vision of atonement, see Rebecca Ann Parker and Rita Nakashima Brock, *Saving Paradise* (Boston: Beacon Press, 2009).

with the One who loved us into life and who loves us toward wholeness, beauty, and adventure in each moment of experience.

Process theology emphasizes Christmas (incarnation) and Easter (resurrection and new life) as well as Good Friday (the cross) in understanding Jesus' mission. In the spirit of Christmas, process theology affirms that revelation is both universal and personal. God's healing power and wisdom are implicitly at work in all things, including a Jewish working class family, soon to become political refugees. Further, God's incarnational energy, personally and uniquely present in Jesus, may be experienced in many diverse ways, depending on the need or the context. The true light, coming into the world, enlightens all things.

The intersection of Good Friday and Easter reveals the lively power of divine possibility. Death and suffering are not final, but may be transformed and revitalized through God's aim at creative transformation. There are no absolute dead ends in the process understanding of God's saving work in Jesus Christ. Resurrection reflects life's growing edge, bursting forth unexpectedly when we are overwhelmed by forces of destruction beyond our control. In a world of lively and emerging creativity, Christians will not seek to understand fully the resurrection narratives; rather, they will seek to experience resurrection life in the struggles of everyday personal, professional, and political life.

Universal Christ. Emerging process theology affirms that God seeks healing and salvation in all things and through many media, not just the Christian tradition.

Christians can affirm that God is present in Christ in a saving and healing way without denying divine revelation and salvation in other religious traditions. Conversely, honoring the wisdom of Buddha, the Dalai Lama, or Mohammed in no way diminishes the life-transforming relationship we have in communion with Jesus. The presence of world religions, accordingly, is not a result of human sin, ignorance, or pride, but reflects God's inspiration in every culture. In the divine-human adventure, God provides insights and energy appropriate not only for each moment of experience, but for the world's diverse cultures and religious traditions. Today's global spirituality provides a unique opportunity for mutual enrichment and growth among the world's religions. As John Cobb affirms, "Christ is the Way that excludes no Way." The Christ consciousness and healing energy that defined Jesus' experience of call and response is not confined to one healing tradition or one stream of faith. Jesus comes to us intimately and personally in ways that respond to our deepest needs.

My former colleague at Lancaster Theological Seminary Lee Barrett uses the word "Jesai" as a way to describe the many ways Jesus has been understood throughout history. Process theology also affirms that the reality and experience of Jesus as Christ is many-faceted. While I focus on the healing as definitive of Jesus' ministry in this text, I believe that Jesus' healing presence flows dynamically through his roles as spirit-person and mediator of divine experience to others, friend of sinners and companion of the marginalized, holistic wisdom and parable teacher, prophet of God's Shalom, transformer of tradition, servant leader, and resurrected one. Jesus embodies, then and now, God's many and diverse aims at abundant life for all creation. These aims are political and economic as well as personal.

Process theology sees our understanding of Jesus' ministry and relationship with God as profoundly interconnected and complementary. The good news of healing hospitality, welcoming of outcasts and marginalized persons; personal transformation across social boundaries; healing community and healing touch; and God-awareness that was at the heart of Jesus' ministry is of one piece with an inclusive life-changing, global, and embodied Christology which embraces today's emerging visions of Christian faith. Through awakening to Jesus' transforming energy and the healing power of hospitality, we share in the pathway of Jesus and will do greater things than we can imagine. (John 14:12)

Living Process
An Emerging Spiritual Practice

The healing ministry of Jesus, in its integration of divine power and human response, invites us to affirm the significance of many media of healing, including Western medicine, complementary medicine, liturgical healing, and spiritual practice. In order to experience the healing Christ in your own life, I invite you to set aside some time for quiet prayer and meditation. In the stillness, open yourself to divine insight and healing energy. As a focus, you might ask

God, "Where do I need healing in my life?" Be still and listen for a response, whether an image, word, or insight. As you become aware of an area in need of healing, now take time to ask, "How might I find wholeness in this situation of body, mind, spirit, or relationship?" Once again, listen for divine insights, whether in silence, a synchronous encounter, or scriptural wisdom. Process theology invites us to seek healing in all things and seek God's healing presence in any appropriate avenue of healing.

Chapter Five

Spirit of Gentleness

Spirit, spirit of gentleness, blow through the wilderness, calling and free, Spirit, spirit of restlessness, stir me from placidness, wind on the sea.[26]

A NUMBER OF YEARS AGO, I TAUGHT a course on the healings of Jesus at Wesley Theological Seminary in Washington D.C. We concluded the class with a healing service. When the first student came up for the laying on of hands and healing prayer, I touched her forehead and down she went, "slain in the spirit." Luckily, she was caught by a fellow classmate. Needless to say, as a progressive professor at a mainstream United Methodist seminary, I was surprised and stunned. Wishing to preserve my reputation in the academic world, I prayed that my students would keep this manifestation of the Holy Spirit to themselves! Although I have not had such an experience since that time, I have come to believe that God's Spirit moves in surprising and sometimes dramatic

---

[26] Jim Manley, "Spirit of Gentleness." Used by permission.

as well as gentle ways, to transform our lives and provide the spiritual nurture we need.

Jim Manley's "Spirit of Gentleness" captures the essence of process theology's understanding of the God's Holy Spirit. The Spirit manifests God's intimate presence in our lives and planetary history. The One God's multi-faceted Spirit both nurtures and challenges. It comforts the weary and gives them a second wind as they lean toward God's growing edges in our world. But, it also challenges the complacent to "stride toward freedom" and justice for all creation. God's spirit speaks in "sighs too deep for words" in the depths of our experience, and joins our heart-felt yearnings with the groaning of creation toward wholeness. (Romans 8:18-27)

An emerging vision of process theology affirms the importance of spirit-centered progressive theology. Sadly, many mainstream and progressive Christians omit the movements of God's Spirit in their understanding of God's presence in human life. In our focus on the oneness of God, we often neglect to affirm that divine unity is also lively, complex, and multi-faceted. Further, the association of manifestations of the Holy Spirit with charismatic and Pentecostal Christianity raises issues of conservative theology and non-rational experiences that trouble certain progressive Christians. Still, as John's gospel proclaims, "the wind [or spirit] blows where it chooses, and you hear the sound of it, and you do not know where it comes from or where it goes. So it is with everyone who is born of the Spirit." (John 3:8-9) Living in the Spirit calls us to let go of our agendas and open to surprising, challenging, and life-transforming possibilities for ourselves and for the planet. Living in the Spirit truly calls us to create our theologies, practices, and faith communities as we go along by opening our eyes to the unexpected movements of God's Spirit, within the church and wherever "two or three," or even one, are gathered.

Looking back at your own religious journey, can you recall the last time a mainstream or progressive Christian minister preached a lively sermon, invoking the presence of the Holy Spirit in the life of the church and Christian spiritual formation? When was the last time you heard a theologically insightful sermon on the Trinity? What was the heart of the message of the "threeness" of God?

Scandalized by what they see as the emotional excesses of contemporary Pentecostal Christianity, most vividly represented by the prosperity gospel movement that assumes a direct connection between faith, health, and riches, and the antics of televangelists and faith healers, many mainstream and progressive Christians have neglected and even rejected any constructive reflection on God's Holy Spirit. The signs and wonders of the Holy Spirit, described throughout Acts of the Apostles, and especially in the first two chapters of Acts, have been consigned by many mainstream and progressive Christians to the outmoded and irrelevant three story universe of the ancient world. Unpredictable, mysterious, and trans-rational in nature, the movements of the Holy Spirit do not conform to the modern world's quest for comprehension and control, whether affirmed by rationalist liberals or literalist conservatives. If the Spirit truly "blows where it chooses," then we must, as

Annie Dillard suggests, put on our crash helmets and strap ourselves to the pews, for we're in for a wild spiritual ride!

However we understand the movements of God's Spirit, the Spirit has an uncanny way of driving us beyond narrow rationalism to explore the surprises and mysteries of the universe within and beyond human experience. God's Spirit invites all of us to be mystics and healers, who see God's hand in all creation and then reach out to be God's partners in embracing, healing, and liberating the many embodiments of God's Spirit in the non-human world. If we truly open to God's Spirit of possibility, then we must be prepared to follow the counsel of the marquee of a congregation in Lancaster, Pennsylvania that sold its building in order to move to another location, "the Spirit said move, and so we did!"

In a time in which many persons seek something more than ownership, control, and power, process theology asks progressive, mainstream, and open and relational evangelical Christians to consider: the following questions: *Can we and our churches become spirit-centered in our responses to the spiritual, economic, and ecological challenges of the twenty-first century? Can we claim a vision of the Spirit that fills us with Pentecostal fervor to heal the planet and awakens us to unexpected possibilities for life-changing spiritual experiences?*

Too often, mainstream and progressive Christians expect too little from God and too little from themselves. Contrary to the breadth of our theological affirmations, our experiential world has often been too small and our loyalties have often been too narrow, confined solely to the nation, the human species, or a particular religious vision. Attuned to the movements of the Spirit breathing in our lives and all creation, we can imagine great possibilities, open to holy energies, and embody these possibilities in our daily personal and congregational lives. We can be part of a world of wonders, in which "miracles," surprising moments of divine power in our lives and communities, are both expected and accepted!

Openness to God's Spirit makes possible the occurrence of signs and wonders, grounded in God's movements in the natural world that go beyond our expectations. Attentiveness to God's spirit calls us to open "the doors of perception" (William Blake) to unseen realities and subtle energies and to trust God's transforming spirit moving in our hearts, minds, and hands. Progressive Christianity's uneasiness and ignorance of popular Pentecostalism holds within in it an invitation to discover our own lively and open-spirited Progressive Pentecosts – science affirming, medically sound, politically committed, ecologically transformative, mystically sensitive, and spiritually adventurous.

Rabbi Abraham Joshua Heschel asserted that experiences of "radical amazement" are at the heart of the spiritual adventure. Those who turn their hearts toward God's Spirit discover a world of surprise and adventure, a world in which divine wisdom is reflected in the smallest of molecules and the grandest of galaxies. On the day of resurrection, Jesus mysteriously appeared in the company of his followers and gave them their mission, "Peace be with you. As [God] has sent me, so I send you." And, then, "Jesus breathed on them and said to them, 'Receive the Holy Spirit.'" Jesus worked within the natural processes of respiration - energizing, reviving, transforming, empowering, and inspiring his followers to go out into the world as healers, teachers, and liberators. Jesus is still breathing in our lives.

Take a moment right now to breathe deeply. As you breathe, imagine Jesus breathing in and through you. Imagine each breath filling you with God's spirit, imagine the whole world breathing in synch with God's spirit. What does it feel like to inhale with Jesus and to experience God's spirit breathing within you and inspiring you with every new breath? What does it feel like to inhale Jesus' very breath as your deepest reality?

Returning to the post-resurrection narratives, just weeks after resurrection day, according to another spirit story recorded in Acts 2, wind and flame enveloped Jesus' earliest followers, inspiring them to speak and hear the good news, despite differences in ethnicity and race. In contrast to those who restrict God's Spirit to congregational life or a particular spiritual manifestation, the miracle of Pentecost joined intimacy with universality. Everyone receives a revelation; everyone reveals divine wisdom; and everyone shares in a surprising holy adventure.

> I will pour out my spirit upon all flesh, and your sons and your daughters shall prophesy, and your young men shall see visions, and your old men shall dream dreams. Even upon my

slaves, both men and
women, I will pour out my
Spirit; and they shall
prophesy." (Acts 2;17-18)

In response to the lively movements of God's
Spirit on the day of Pentecost, "awe came upon everyone,
because many wonders and signs were being done by the
apostles." (Acts 2:43) Once again, God's spirit
energetically works within the lives of a community,
using the gifts of God residing within the many
community members. The Pentecost manifestation of
God's Spirit reminds us that God's energetic power is also
ours and that we are called to "greater works" as the
Spirit's companions than we can imagine in transforming
our relationships, congregations, and this good earth.
(John 14:12) As our inner advocate and helper, the Spirit
abides in us, inspiring us to seek the healing of creation.

Process theology's spirit-centered naturalism
enlivens and enlightens our experience of wonders within
the world of interdependent, naturalistic causation, and
heightens the impact of God's presence in our lives. The
whole earth, human and non-human, sacred and secular,
Christian and non-Christian, is, at its depths, "full of
God's glory." (Isaiah 6:3) When the Psalmist proclaims
"let everything that breathes praise God" (Psalm 150:6),
this ancient spirit guide reminds us that every creature
reveals God's lively Spirit at its depths. The Spirit
breathes through the joy of a boy playing with a fox
terrier, the blinking of fireflies, and purring of a Siamese
cat, and your own dreams and visions.

In contrast to Enlightenment deism and conservative supernaturalism, both of which are grounded in the belief that God operates from "outside" the world, intruding occasionally in ways that subvert nature's regularity, process theology affirms that God's Spirit moves within all things, inviting us and them to be "more" than they or we can imagine.

During our son's two weeks of hospitalization, following his diagnosis of cancer, I observed God's Spirit moving in the prayers and visits of friends from across the United States. Often I experienced more of the "church" among twenty-something seekers than in congregational worship. One afternoon, I felt the Spirit move as six twenty-something friends gathered around Matt's bedside. None but Matt attended church; but I felt the Spirit of love abounding in hugs and laughter. On that particular day, as Matt's friends sat at his bedside, all of six received cell phone calls in the space of two minutes from friends asking how Matt was doing. The Spirit's open source network of love moved through that space and across the planet, healing and connecting, manifesting herself in the lives of six friends, none of whom would call her or himself Christian.

Spirit-centered progressive Christianity inspires experiences of awe and wonder as we consider the universe in all of its fourteen billion year, hundred billion galaxy journey; the gentle emergence and evolution of life-forms out of primordial chaos; the pivotal moments of spiritual transformation that gave birth to the great religious traditions of the world and still give birth to our own spiritual adventures; and the lure toward tomorrow that challenges the entropy of institutions, powers, and principalities. Spirit-centered faith begins with a sense of God's movements in our lives, communities, and the world and spirals outward in acts of generosity, healing, and justice for all creation.

Acts 2 portrays a faithful and protean community that lives by the spirit, letting go of go of individual self-centeredness to embrace the deeper self-centeredness of living by the Spirit.

> All who believed were together and had all things in common; they would sell their possessions and goods and distribute the proceeds to all, as any had need. Day by day, as they spent much time together in the temple, they broke bread at home and ate their food with glad and generous hearts, praising God and having the goodwill of all the people. And day by day God added to their number those who were being saved. (Acts 2:44-47)

Once more, take a moment to breathe deeply and read the words from Acts 2:44-47 again. Experience their holistic integration of theological reflection, spiritual practice, hospitality, and social conscience. Where do these words call you in your own emerging faith? Where do you need to embrace a larger experience of God's spirit in your life and relationships? Where does your theology need to become embodied in simple acts of connection and hospitality?

105

As I've noted throughout this text, emerging process theology affirms a generous vision of divine revelation that reaches far beyond human experience to embrace the whole earth and the mysterious and ambient universe beyond. Creation groans in its quest for wholeness, inspiring the first spirit-centered followers of the way of Jesus to see themselves as God's partners in healing the world, not from the outside but in the very ordinary creaturely acts of singing, praying, eating, and sharing. Present in the first moments of creation, this same spirit leads us forward to new and holy adventures of world transformation. Once again, let Jim Manley's process-inspired words guide our theological reflection.

> You moved on the waters, you called to the deep, then you coaxed up the mountains from the valleys of sleep;
>
> And over the eons you called to each thing, "Awake from your slumbers and rise on your wings."....
>
> You call from tomorrow, you break ancient schemes, from the bondage of sorrow the captives dream dreams;
>
> Our women see visions, our men clear their eyes, With bold new decisions your people arise.

Now, listen quietly to the lively global vision of God's spirit portrayed in Paul's Letter to the Romans, Chapter 8:

> We know that the whole creation has been groaning in labor pains until now; and not only the creation, but we ourselves who have the first fruits of the Spirit, groan inwardly while we wait for adoption, the redemption of our bodies....the Spirit helps us in our weakness; for we do not know how to pray as we ought, but that very Spirit intercedes with sighs too deep for words. (Romans 8:22-23, 26)

Imagine a spirit-filled world! Imagine God's spirit, breathing in and through all things, giving them life, energy, *chi*, *ki*, *prana*, *ruach*, and inviting them to evolve toward the wholeness in God's realm of shalom, beauty, and love.

Process theology invites us to be part of this global Spirit story, to let the Spirit's creative wisdom breathe in us, and move us toward images of future hope with open hearts, lively imaginations, and healing hands. The Spirit's story is larger than church story or the human story, but encompasses creation in all of its wonder and complexity. Filled with the Spirit, we can truly expect signs, wonders, and acts of power in the daily lives of congregations and persons. God is here, Spirit moves, Life abounds, and no one is left out!

Wholly Trinity

Despite the language of their denominational worship books and worship services, many progressive and mainstream Christians, including pastors, are functionally Unitarian in theology in their focus on God as Creator and Actor in the universe. In this context, an emerging process theology can be a resource for transforming and renewing our images of the trinity in a pluralistic age. Process theology sees God as "wholly trinity," a lively, dynamic, interdependent center of dancing relatedness, always one, yet never finished in God's quest for lively transformation.

Emerging process theologians see the trinity as a reflection of the many-faceted nature and experience of God. Infinite in experience and imagination, the God of all things cannot be limited by one image, word, or belief system. While one in spirit and experience, God is the creative energy and vision of the universe in its entirety and each moment; the embodied healer and wisdom giver to humankind; and the inspiration for the healing of creation. God is a constantly evolving process of creative transformation, bringing together the one and many in God's experience and in the ongoing process of personal and global creativity. God's many-faceted nature embraces the contrasts of time and eternity, intimacy and universality, perpetual perishing and everlasting life, pain and healing, and unity and plurality. The many-faceted wholly trinity gives birth to a variety of divine revelations, intimately addressing each creature and culture, as well as one global movement toward wholeness and transformation. The affirmation of divine trinity invites us to see God as three, although holistically speaking more than three, personally inspiring each moment of experience, whose oneness gives birth to cosmic variety beyond our comprehension.

In imagining trinity, we once more join both the *kataphatic* and *apophatic* ways of Christian experience. Wholly trinity points to revelation everywhere and in everything, to God's breath in our breath, and God's light in all light. Wholly trinity also points beyond itself to the God who is always beyond word, deed, and sacrament. The wind blowing where it will can be glimpsed but never captured by our theologies and practices, only gratefully embraced in its wondrous complexity and mystery.

Still, the vision of trinity calls us to imaginative here and now theological reflection. Proverbs 8:22-31 expresses the dynamic and delightful dance of creation, birthing forth from God's wholly trinity. As God birthed forth this universe, the many-faceted God created with Wisdom, Sophia, as God's intimate "companion":

> When God marked out the foundations of the earth, then I was beside God like a *playful and creative child*' and I was daily God's delight, rejoicing before God always, rejoicing in God's inhabited world and delighting in the human race." (Proverbs 8:29b-31)

Take a moment to read these words again. Put away the headlines from the newspaper or cable news for a moment. While not denying the violence, injustice, and threat is tragically part of our world, imagine God playfully creating the world. Imagine the diverse and colorful intricacy of creation bursting forth at both the galactic and cellular levels.   Imagine Holy/Wholly Wisdom, Sophia, playfully beckoning you to be part of the wonder-full dance of creation in its many manifestations.

A many-faceted God is beyond and within the distinctions of gender and ethnicity. Although words "let us create humankind in our image....male and female" (Genesis 1:26-27) will always remain mysterious, surely they point to a lively, evolving reality that creates from its imagination, embraces change and complexity, and dearly loves all that comes into being. From this perspective, the language of the trinity always points beyond itself and cannot be contained by words such as "Father, Son, and Holy Spirit" or "Creator, Redeemer, and Sustainer." The one God surely acts in many ways and is known by many names, all reflecting divine revelation, all insufficient to describe the Wholly One , Wholly Three, Wholly Loving Reality. While my own personal preference in describing the trinity joins tradition and novelty – "Father, Son, and Holy Spirit; Creator, Healer [or Redeemer], and Inspirer [or Sustainer] of us all" – even these words barely touch the awesome and wonder-full everlasting and ever-present God. Process theology invites us to see the trinity in spirit-centered ways, pushing beyond our known images to a holy and imaginative adventure in which we discover "God in all things" and "all things in God."   Emerging process theology challenges us, to "bring many names" for God's nature and relationship with us to worship and prayer. A lively understanding of trinity affirms many names and excludes no healing name, as hymn writer Brian Wren suggests, awakening us to holiness in icon, metaphor, art, poetry, and media, as we trace the ever-free and diverse movements of God's spirit bringing forth diverse forms of beauty in our world.[27]

Living Process
An Emerging Spiritual Practice

This week, take time to breathe with God's Spirit. Imagine that you are inhaling the same breath that Jesus bestowed upon his followers. Visualize yourself "receiving the Holy Spirit" as you let God's spirit permeate every cell and every thought. Feel God's Spirit as your deepest reality.

Throughout the day, inhale and then exhale God's Spirit as your gift of healing interdependence to those around you. Pause and notice God's Spirit in your human and non-human companions. Give thanks for the universal, yet intimate, inspiring presence of God's Spirit in the world.

---

[27] Brian Wren, "Bring Many Names."

Chapter Six

Emerging Universe

Let everything that breathes, praise God!
Praise God!" (Psalm 150:6)

"Holy, Holy, Holy, is the God of Hosts;
the whole earth is full of God's glory.
(Isaiah 6:3)

For creation waits with eager longing for
the revealing of the children of God....We
know that the whole creation has been
groaning in labor pains until now; and not
only the creation, but we ourselves, who
have the first fruits of the Spirit, groan
inwardly while we wait for adoption, the
redemption of our bodies. (Romans 8:20-
23)

IN THE SMALL TOWN OF DOVER, NOT far from our home
in Lancaster, Pennsylvania, Christians fought one another
over whether or not intelligent design, a form of faith-
based science advocating the vision of a divinely-created
purpose driven universe in which God created all the

species "in the beginning," should be taught as an alternative to the theory of evolution. A large faction of the community saw evolutionary theory as a godless threat to their values and faith. They assumed that the biblical accounts of creation found in the first two chapters of Genesis literally and infallibly described the creation of the earth and its species, and that anything contrary to their understanding of the biblical creation story was both scientifically inaccurate and spiritually dangerous. To these Christians, persons of faith had to choose between science and scripture, and when science and scripture are in apparent conflict with one another, God's written words from Genesis must always prevail over secular science.

Another segment of the community saw no conflict between Christianity and evolution, broadly understood, and objected to only one vision of faith, the biblical creationist model, being taught to their children. They recognized a diversity of pathways to truth within Christianity and in the larger culture. They wanted a "both/and" approach to the dialogue of science and faith.

While I do not dispute the good faith of those who wish to have Genesis taught as scientific theory in public school classrooms, I believe that proponents of scientific creationism and intelligent design turn their backs on the best current scientific thinking by: their denial of evidence supporting the theory of evolution and their belief that the scientific method must be subservient to literal interpretations of the Bible in understanding the universe. In their advocacy of "intelligent design," they neglect to follow the movements of Creative Wisdom that inspire

114

the quest for truth whether it occurs in the scientific laboratory, operating room, archeological dig, or in the reading of scripture and acts of public worship, as well as Divine Wisdom in the patient evolution of the universe in all its planetary and species diversity.

In light of the ongoing battles between "creation" and "evolution," I believe that Christian dialogue with science and culture has been undermined by the uncritical perception that biblical literalists speak for the majority of Christians. To counteract this perception, often in the course of a guest sermon or lecture, I point out the interplay of the cosmic and the personal aspects of faith by noting that our lives as faithful people are rooted "in a fourteen billion year and hundred billion galaxy cosmic adventure." My goal is to remind the congregants that the biblical witness is intended to be the beginning of our spiritual adventure and not the final word on our understanding of ourselves and the world.

While biblical literalists appropriately seek something constant in a world of change, their quest for certainty has led to them to create a schism between faith and science in which many Christians have consistently chosen to be on the losing side of controversies involving scientific exploration and biblical interpretation. Emerging process theology presents an alternative vision, open to the many understandings of creation as metaphors, each contributing to a many-faceted holistic and meaningful vision of our emerging and evolving cosmos and human adventure.

Inspired by the lively and creative wisdom of the Prologue of John's Gospel (most especially John 1:1-5, 9,

115

14), emerging process theology sees revelation and creation as universal, albeit personal and variable. Persons can experience divine inspiration in laboratories, surgical theatres, observatories, and fossil fields. Process theology affirms one of the cardinal tenets of early Christian Logos theology, the affirmation that wherever truth is present, even outside of Christianity, God is its source. Accordingly, in the spirit of the chapter on Jesus the Healer, I affirm "wherever truth, healing, and open-minded scientific exploration are present, even outside of Christianity, God is its source."

Emerging process theology avoids the extremes of scientific materialism and theistic supernaturalism. On the one hand, process theology questions any view of the universe that denies the universality of value, inspiration, creativity, and purpose. Discovering traces of creative wisdom or divine intelligence in naturally occurring processes in no way undermines the scientific method. Process theologians affirm that the evolving universe reveals the movements of a Creative Wisdom that works patiently and persuasively throughout the fourteen billion year cosmic adventure. On the other hand, process theologians resist identifying scriptural literalism with scientific truth and supernaturalism with divine creativity. Like all vehicles of revelation, scripture is time-bound, relative, and imperfect, despite its power to transform our spiritual lives. The biblical passages from Genesis do not describe the age of the earth or the intricacies of cosmic evolution, but proclaim the presence of a creative, life-giving, and intelligent spirit, moving within each stage of the cosmic and human adventures. The biblical tradition describes a lively and inspired universe in which the interplay of order and novelty, structure and creativity, give birth to adventure and freedom in our spiritual lives and in the planetary journey.

Emerging process theology also challenges "scientism," the belief that reality is confined to what can be observed through the scientific method or described fully in terms of non-purposive and entirely physical natural causes. The universe of quarks, black holes, and dancing galaxies is more beautiful than we can imagine. Our own quest for knowledge of the universe reflects a deep and universal wisdom which guides cells, solar systems, and galaxies.

Reflecting the creative movements of a generous and abundant God, the universe abounds in diversity. Far from being the easily disposable "front porch of eternity," creation is the reflection of divine activity and the mirror of God's glory. Everlasting life is revealed in each passing moment as well as in the adventure of life beyond the grave.

The words of Romans 8 suggest that creation is leaning toward the future. God is still creating and the universe is still emerging, aiming toward the wholeness of God's shalom. Far from denying God's power and wisdom, process theology sees divine handiwork in the dynamic, interdependence of life on this planet and throughout the universe. Wonder and reverence are appropriate responses to a universe that birthed nearly fourteen billion years ago and from whose creative adventure has sprung forth perhaps one hundred billion galaxies, each with a billion solar systems like our own.

With the Psalmist, we recognize the contrast between our insignificance on the world stage and God's intimate presence in the human adventure.

> O God, our Sovereign, how majestic is
> your name in all the earth!...
>
> When I look at your heavens, the work of
> your fingers,
>
> The moon and the stars you have
> established;
>
> What are human beings that you are
> mindful of them,
> Mortals that you care for them?
>
> Yet you have made them a little lower than
> the divine beings,
>
> And crowned them with glory and honor.
> (Psalm 8:1, 3-5)

Emerging process theology calls us beyond human-centered and earth-centered visions of reality. God is in all things, including the human and earth adventures, but God's care also encompasses every solar system and galaxy. God is present in all creation, luring it forward on its evolutionary journey, just as God is luring humankind forward in light of God's dream of shalom. God has a vision; indeed God has many visions, for the non-human world that God loves deeply. God's care ranges far beyond the earth and its inhabitants. The Hubble telescope reveals the dancing of galaxies and the rising and perishing of suns. We must proclaim the wonder of our own human being, while confessing that we can discern only a fraction of God's handiwork in our solar system and the home galaxy we call the Milky Way. While process theology remains agnostic about the existence and nature of life forms on other planets, the reality of galaxies and solar systems beyond our imagination gives us reason to believe that life emerges in varied forms as a result of God's patient inspiration, creativity, and companionship. Further, our own quests to follow God's emerging vision of humankind challenge us to recognize that we are not the crown of creation or final chapter of God's holy adventure, even on this planet. As humans, we too are in process and should we escape human-influenced and chosen cataclysms such as global climate change, nuclear winter, and biological plague, new and more highly evolved forms of humanity may emerge on this planet or as we crisscross our galaxy in the centuries to come. In what some cosmologists describe as a multi-centered universe, we can claim to be at the center of the universe while acknowledging that every other planet and solar system is also at the center of an evolving universe.

God's creative wisdom is moving through all things. God has a vision, personal, planetary, and cosmic, but this wise vision emerges in an ongoing call and response at every level of the universe, part and whole.

Evolution and Divine Power. One of the most cited arguments against theistic understandings of evolution is

119

that the fourteen billion year evolutionary journey challenges traditional understandings of divine power and the reality of evil. According to many traditional Christian theologies, whether in their mainstream, evangelical, or scientific creationist forms, God created the universe out of nothing *(ex nihilo)* entirely in accord with God's all-powerful will. From their perspective, the universe has a definite beginning and will eventually be destroyed according to God's pre-ordained timetable. God infallibly knows and has programmed every detail of the earth's history without our input, as Rick Warren asserts. In such a universe, nothing new truly happens, nor do creaturely actions contribute anything ultimately positive to God's plan for the universe.

Traditional understandings of divine power see God's unilateral power as all-encompassing. Yet, despite their affirmation of the doctrine of divine omnipotence, traditional Christians also believe that sin enters the world as the result of human decision-making "once upon a time." Though they believe that humans caused the fall of humankind and creation, traditional theologies recognize that God must have known about it in advance and, therefore, either: 1) caused the tragic fall of humankind, permitting such a devastating decision to occur, or 2) did nothing to prevent the universal scope of its impact on creation.

Emerging process theologians challenge the doctrine of "original sin" in light of their understanding of "original goodness" or "original wholeness" of creation and human life as reflective of God's creative wisdom. The biblical narrative of the creation of humankind and subsequent human history portrays the creative process as a dynamic and evolving divine call and human response in which God experiences both the joy and pain of the world. The many-faceted biblical narrative reflects the constantly creative movements of a compassionate God who seeks to bring forth a just society and beautiful world in the context of the positive and negative impact of human freedom.

In an interdependent creative universe, process theology sees the "fall of humankind" as testimony to the interplay of divine call and creaturely response. "Adam" and "Eve" do not give up following their "act of disobedience," but go forth from Eden, lured by divine creativity, to begin new adventures. Perhaps, the mythical first couple's act of disobedience was not so much a violation of divine law but a premature and self-centered expression of human creativity and curiosity.

The evolutionary process in all its wonder and ambiguity gives evidence to a call forward, rather than the downward plunge into chaos and entropy. Evolution testifies to competition among species, but it also testifies to cooperation among species, in the evolutionary advance. Accordingly, a multi-billion year evolutionary process reflects God's generosity and compassion for creatures both simple and complex, and God's willingness to work with, rather than condemn imperfections, both human and non-human, even when creaturely decisions slow down the progress of God's emerging and evolving vision of the future. God's creative wisdom always seeks the best response in every situation and though our behaviors may lead to a diminishment of divine activity in the present moment, God continues to inspire movements toward beauty and creativity in every person and the planet as a whole. God never gives up on the universe, our planet, or humankind.

In its vision of personal and planetary evolution, emerging process theology defines divine power in terms of multi-faceted relationship and persuasion rather than unilateral omnipotence. The multi-billion year process of cosmic and planetary evolution reflects God's compassionate care and persistent aim at beauty, best described by the Genesis' image of continuous creation out of an aboriginal chaos and throughout planetary history.[28] The God who brings forth this universe through the big birth of creation is constantly creating, luring forth new forms of experience and life, and new forms of divine-creaturely partnership. God is truly "mighty," though not "almighty" in God's unending creativity. God's creativity works within every moment and every epoch to bring novelty into the universe from age to age and generation to generation. Though God's power is not omnipotent, it is infinite insofar as the divine-creaturely partnership at every level presents God's creation with ever new and unending possibilities of creativity and artistry.

Emerging process theology does not give us the mechanics of evolution, but it gives us a framework for seeing the evolutionary process as the interplay of creative intelligence and creaturely responsiveness. Emerging

---

[28] Catherine Keller, *Face of the Deep: A Theology of Becoming* (London: Routledge, 2003).

process theology also gives us a broad ethical framework, given our place in a lively, enchanted universe. Divine handiwork, reflected in a living universe, invites us to have reverence for life in all its myriad forms and calls us to become conscious partners not only in healing the earth but in bringing forth God's shalom in our world. Our mission is to be God's partners in the next stages of God's holy adventure on Planet Earth!

Living Process
An Emerging Spiritual Practice

Process theology sees divine creativity as the energy of evolution. The energy of evolution is personal as well as global. God is working in our lives to bring forth greater beauty and complexity of experience. We are part of the evolutionary process and, as conscious participants and partners with God's creative wisdom, we can share in God's holy adventure of emerging creativity.

Take some time to be still in God's presence. Breathe deeply the energies of God, flowing in all things. Feel God's creative energy filling your whole being. Feel God's creativity calling you forward to new adventures of self and planetary creation. As you inhale and exhale, feel your connection with all things as both a receiver and a giver. Experience God's light, described in John 1:1-5, 9, flowing in and through you to all creation.

Now, in the silence consider the following question, "where am I called to be God's partner in the evolution of our planet to new forms of life and beauty?" Begin to live and act upon the insights you receive.

Chapter Seven

The Church as Healing Community

IF ONE MEMBER SUFFERS, ALL SUFFER together with it; if one member is honored, all rejoice together with it. Now you are the body of Christ and individually members of it.[29]

Recently as we began worship at our congregation Disciples United Community Church (DUCC), I found myself happily amazed as I looked over the bulletin.[30] In the course of one worship service, members of this avowedly progressive, process-oriented church, sang hymns and songs from Mexico, Finland, North America, Iona in Scotland, and South Africa; played drums and tambourines; reflected in an interactive manner on the God's universal love and revelation; celebrated communion with a five year old child sharing the bread and cup; and concluded with a healing service involving laying on of hands and reiki healing touch. The spirit flowed as we experienced God's presence through every

---

[29] I Corinthians 12:26-27

[30] For more information on Disciples United Community Church, where I served as co-pastor from 2004-2010, see www.ducc.us.

sense, including the flavor of homemade bread at the potluck supper that followed worship. Our community's worship reflects the lively, multi-sensory, global and interactive spirit, characteristic of today's emerging Christian communities.

In Chapters Four and Five, we described the traits of a spirit-centered faith, grounded in the ministry of Jesus and the works of the Holy Spirit. In this chapter, we focus on the church as a spirit-centered healing community, reflecting the interplay of divine call and human response in Jesus' healing ministry and our own lives. While we suspect that the "honeymoon" of the church described throughout the Acts of the Apostles was a fleeting experience, Acts presents the vision of a spiritually-vital, life-transforming, and world-changing faith. The church as healing community, grounded in God's revelation in the experience of the Hebraic community and early church, reflects God's concern for every aspect of the well-being of social groups as well as individuals.

Acts of the Apostles describes what an emerging church would be like if we truly believed we could experience and achieve "greater things" than those who were the first companions of the One whose love inspired the Christian adventure. (John 14:12) Today, emerging process theology calls progressive Christians to imagine great things, precisely because we, like the earliest followers of Jesus, live in perilous times, in which the fate of the planet is jeopardized by global climate change, international violence, economic uncertainty, and a growing body of Christians and followers of other faith traditions, who see "salvation" in terms of destruction rather than new creation. The voice of life-affirming, inclusive, and dynamic Christianity seems but a whisper, when compared to the strident voices of those Christians for whom the bad news of planetary destruction signals the good news of Christ's immanent return; nationalistic foreign policy reflects God's will; and who promote a prosperity gospel while creation is groaning under the threat of ecological catastrophe. The voice of life-affirming emerging Christianity is needed now more than ever as the inspiration and catalyst for a faith that heals both persons and the planet.

Emerging process theology is unabashedly progressive and global in its orientation, whether its primary manifestation is found among spirit-centered progressives or open-spirited evangelicals. Those of us who claim to be progressive Christians know that the hour is late for our churches, the faith of the prophets and Jesus, and the planet upon which we live.

As we look at the current state of North American Christianity, process theologians call us to ask ourselves the following questions: *Can Christianity become good news for persons who have been marginalized, suffered abuse, or experienced trauma as a result of their social standing, sexual identity, or economic status? Can emerging process theology provide a welcoming pathway to a robust, spirit-centered, and planet-transforming faith?*

Hope and healing are at the heart of emerging process theology. Process theology affirms that God provides both a vision of possibilities and the energy to achieve that vision in every moment of experience and over the long stretch of history. God seeks abundant life for all creation, and not just the privileged few. Reflecting God's vision of shalom, the healer Jesus sought transformation and abundant life for persons and communities alike. While the church has seldom measured up to God's vision of shalom, emerging process theology sees the church as an agile and protean community of personal and social wholeness and transformation, creatively embracing diversity within the dynamic unity of the body of Christ. Like the earliest followers of Jesus, described in Acts of the Apostles, today's emerging Christians are called to make it up as we go along, creatively transforming ancient rituals and traditions and global spiritualities and practices in light of God's evolving present and future visions. Emerging Christian communities are both "spiritual" and "religious" in their dynamic and shape-shifting integration of spontaneity and structure, experience and theological reflection, and innovation and tradition. Such lively holistic faith communities embody what emerging church theologian-pastor Doug Pagitt describes as "a Christianity worth believing."[31]

An Emerging Missional Faith. Today, process theology calls for the emergence of a 21st century "confessing church," in the spirit of those who German Christians who challenged the powers and principalities of Holocaust Germany and its complacent and often complicit religious leadership. Nothing less than the fate

---

[31] Doug Pagitt, *A Christianity Worth Believing* (San Francisco: Jossey-Bass, 2008).

of the earth is at stake; sadly the earth's greatest enemies are often to be found among those who call themselves Christian. An emerging process relational church embraces the spirit of Pentecost, the heart-felt faith of open-spirited evangelicals, the lively quests of unchurched youth and their parents, and the planetary hopes of progressive Christianity. It also embraces with open hearts and open arms the gifts of the GLBT community and the wisdom of other faith traditions.

While all congregations are concrete, finite, limited, and imperfect, vital and emerging faith communities reflect God's quest to join ancient truths and future visions in a dynamic, ever-evolving now. Process theology sees the church as the "body of Christ," characterized by the interplay of inspiration, interconnectedness, and imagination. Accordingly, process theologians see I Corinthians 12 as a portrait of living, dynamic organism, inspired by the "mind" or "spirit" of Christ. The apostle Paul describes God's intimate and inspiring presence in the church with these words:

Now there are varieties of gifts, but the same Spirit; and there are varieties of services, but the same Christ; and there are varieties of activities but it is the same God who activates all of them in everyone. To each is given the manifestation of the Spirit for the common good. (I Corinthians 12:4-7)

Everyone in the body of Christ reflects God's lively presence. Everyone is gifted, reflecting the divine inspiration and holy vocation in her or his unique way. God's abundance is manifest in diversity, rather than

129

uniformity; and in community rather than individuality. The church reflects God's healing vision when it nurtures both the gifts of its members and the gifts of persons outside the church doors for the well-being of the world.

By definition, the emerging church is missional in nature as it extends the circle of healing from person to faith community to the planet. Its calling is to be a safe environment in which persons can experience God's many gifts in their lives. While personal commitment to God and congregational life are essential both for the health of the community and the possibility for greater manifestations of divine healing energy within and beyond the church, radical hospitality calls us to open the door to everyone without minimal requirements of faith or participation. Grace and love must be unconditional and welcoming, if we are truly to reflect the love that shines upon friend and enemy alike. God wants everyone to have abundant life, not just Christians or active church members.

Recently, I received a prayer request from an occasional participant in our church's worship services. It was prefaced with the words, "I shouldn't be asking for a prayer request since I haven't been to church lately." Her concerns reflect the sense that God's grace and our welcome is contingent on past behavior, commitment, or organizational membership. While we may limit the impact of God's energetic vision for our lives by our actions and beliefs, we can never stop God from seeking abundant life for us and those whom we love. God's quest for abundant life applies to our friends, strangers, and enemies. God's calling for us to seek the common good lures the church from the comfort of the worship space to reach out to least of these, speak truth to power, and follow God's vision of healing the earth.

In the spirit I Corinthians 12, process theology affirms that the church's communal interdependence reflects the interconnectedness of life. When it is true to its mission, the church embodies Jesus' healing ministry in healthy and affirming relationships that extend far beyond its doors. It recognizes that the health of one member shapes the health of the community, and that healthy persons need healthy communities in order to flourish and claim their role as God's healing partners. As the apostle Paul proclaims:

> For just as the body is one and has many members, and all the members of the body, though many, are one body, so it is with Christ. For in one Spirit we were all baptized – Jews or Greeks, slaves or free – and we are all made to drink of one Spirit....If one member suffers, all suffer together with it; if one member is honored, all rejoice together with it. (I Corinthians 12:13-14, 26)

In the healing church, there is truly no "other." Indeed, emerging process theology extends Paul's image of the body of Christ to include the whole earth as well as the faithful community. Although each community member is unique, we are truly one in spirit and flesh. While God seeks wholeness in all things, not just the Christian community, the church's calling is to be mindful of life's interconnectedness as the inspiration to acts of shalom – kindness, healing, and justice. In the spirit of holistic health, process theology envisages the church is a dynamic organism, inspired by the spirit of Christ. But, more than that, the church is embedded in the universe that God is constantly creating. In its affirmation of interdependence and diversity, the mission-inspired church seeks to mediate divine hospitality to all creation. Our quest for personal well-being and our commitment to justice reflect the church's calling to be God's partner in healing the world.

The body of Christ in its most faithful forms is consciously animated by divine energetic imagination, the ever-creative mind of Christ. The church is called to be a community of inspiration, in which persons see each other, despite their imperfections, through the eyes of Christ, and imagine alternative possibilities to the injustice and suffering of the present age. The church most fully embodies its identity when it joins pastoral care with prophetic challenge. In the words of our spiritual parents, "the reformed church is constantly reforming," and the emerging process church is also constantly emerging and transforming itself and the world, in light of Christ's mission. While members are challenged to pause awhile for Sabbath rest, the church is also called to be on the move, expanding its circles of care to include pilgrims and strangers, friends and enemies.

Emerging Process Worship. God encounters us through all the senses. We are called to "taste and see" the goodness of God. We are also called to experience God in smell, touch, and voice. Around the communion table, we pray with our eyes open, discovering God's presence in one another and receiving and giving divine revelations to each other.[32]

Emerging process worship provides the opportunity where persons can receive good bread and good wine, the bread of life and the cup of wholeness that satisfies our thirst for meaning and service. As I write these words, one particular time of worship at Disciples United Community Church (DUCC) is still fresh in my mind. As always, colorful cloth adornments and spiritual symbols transformed a plain multi-purpose room into sacred space. Interactive worship gave voice to each person's experience of God and to the democracy of revelation. Around the table, two children aged five and nine served communion, saying to each person "good bread" and "good juice." Another week, words around the table might be "the bread of life and the cup of healing" or "bread of possibility and the cup of liveliness." Like our parents in the faith, we experience each week's worship as novel, tactile, interactive, and democratic. While we have a pattern to our worship services, worship is always "live," open to the Spirit moving through our own

---

[32] For more on images of global worship, see Bruce Epperly and Daryl Hollinger, *From A Mustard Seed: Enlivening Worship in the Small Church* (Herndon, VA: Alban Institute, 2010).

creativity. Sermons, otherwise known as "reflections," often involve *lectio divina* or a time of wisdom sharing following the preacher's words. God is still speaking in worship, and children and elders can share divine inspiration for just such a time as this.

Small in size, DUCC, like many other emerging communities, is a place where good news is not only heard, but also felt, tasted, touched, and smelled. Emerging process theology invites us throughout the day to "live" the omnipresence of God through commitments to experience God's presence in worship and in every other encounter. Our bidding or intercessory prayer at DUCC proclaims, "God in all things" and "All things in God" as witness to the Creative-Responsive Love "in whom we live and move and have our being."

As they gather for word, table, and worship, emerging communities awaken to the mysterious, yet ever-present God. Our hymns of praise, prayers of intercession and petition, and words of affirmation witness to God's good news, make room for the ever-present God to be more active in our lives and in the world. They bring God's "whispered word," to use a phrase of process theologian Marjorie Suchocki, to conscious experience, so that we might be inspired and guided by God's dream of shalom and planetary wholeness.

The sacraments of baptism and communion inspire us to experience God in all things and enable us to see the whole world as a reflection of God's ever-present love. In the breaking of bread and the sharing of wine, we claim God's "real presence" – God's lively inspiring omnipresence – in the here and now in the midst of celebration and tragedy. In the celebration of communion, the interplay of cross and resurrection, suffering and transformation, reveal the healing power of a Love that embraces every dimension of life in light of God's emerging future. Emerging sacraments truly "save" us; but the salvation they offer is not an escape from hell but an awakening and enhancing of God's healing and wholeness in the here and now. Everlasting life is right where we are – in this holy moment and this holy place.

Today, the mission of emerging process and open-spirited Christianity everywhere is to let its light shine. While we humbly recognize "the falsehood in our own truth," to quote American theologian Reinhold Niebuhr, we must also recognize that we have too often failed to lift our voices for the healing the earth. We have spoken theologically-correct language but often neglected to join healing words with healing acts and prophetic language with prophetic actions. While our calling is not to demonize those within our faith tradition who are hell-bent on planetary destruction, we are challenged as church to live by an alternative vision; one that confronts lies with truth, hate with love, scarcity with abundance, idolatry with prophetic challenge, and polarization with the power and strength of an affirmative vision of God and the world. We are challenged to walk the talk of progressive and emerging process Christianity, even as we share the "good news" of God's creative transformation and healing power.

We can do great things in small as well as larger churches today. We can become lively and protean communities of healing, where persons are soothed, transformed, and energized in body, mind, spirit, and relationships. We can become communities of prayer, awakening ourselves and others to God's vision of planetary healing. We can serve God through prayer, touch, comfort, word, as well as in acts of service in which giver and receiver are joined as God's beloved children as they experience "all things in God." In companionship with a surprising and lively God, our communities can become twenty-first century places of "signs and wonders" that bring healing to seekers, believers, and this good earth.

Living Process
An Emerging Spiritual Practice

The church is called to be a community of imagination in light of God's vision of Shalom. In this spiritual practice, I invite you to visualize a lively healthy body, the "body of Christ." What does this body look like? What are its many parts?

Visualize divine energy flowing through this body, giving life and health to each part. As you look at this energetic body, what body part represents your gifts? Visualize yourself sharing your gifts with the larger body. Now, looking at your part, what parts of the body support your well-being in the body of Christ? Can you personalize the image of the body of Christ by visualizing these parts in terms of your companions in the life of faith? Which persons do you nurture? Which persons nurture your gifts?

Experience this lively bodily energy now flowing forth from the body, transforming the world.

As you conclude this meditation, take time to give thanks for God's presence in the body of Christ and in the world.

Chapter Eight

Life-Transforming Ethics

In a communal religion you study the will of God in order that [God] may preserve you; in a purified religion, you study [God's] Goodness in order to be like [God]. It is the difference between the enemy you conciliate and the companion whom you imitate.[33]

ONE OF THE MOST DIFFICULT EXPERIENCES for an adult child is to make decisions regarding life and death issues related to her or his parent. A month after my eighty six year old father's disabling stroke, his attorney and I met with him to talk about advance directives, that is, the type of medical care that my father wanted to receive should he be unable or incompetent to make these decisions himself. I remember the catch in my throat when I asked my father if he wanted "extraordinary measures" to be used if he were to stop breathing or have another stroke. The questions became more challenging when I asked, "Dad, if you have pneumonia, do you want

---

[33] Alfred North Whitehead, *Religion in the Making*, 40.

to receive antibiotics?" The answer is obvious for a healthy child or adult in midlife, but pneumonia has traditionally been described as the "old person's friend." Without antibiotics to treat the pneumonia, an elder like my father typically experiences a relatively painless death. Although I had taught courses in bioethics and death and dying at Georgetown University School of Medicine, I was now directly faced with the ethical realities that what might be ordinary and obligatory medical care in one situation might become extraordinary, intrusive, and elective in another situation, this time involving my own father.

Today, a handful of states in the United States of America have voted to allow physician-aided death. Using clearly defined procedures, persons with terminal illnesses may receive medical assistance in ending their lives. While once the majority of religious persons believed that only God could end a life, today many persons see matters of life and death as involving human rather than divine decision-making. Many persons are concerned that the medical procedures intended to save their lives will, in fact, prolong their agony and rob them of their personal freedom. They want to be actors rather than victims in responding to matters of life and death. They recognize that medical ethics involves the complexity of concrete persons, with unique sets of values and ailments, and not universal philosophical abstractions.

The holistic and life-affirming theology, characteristic of emerging process theology, joins vision, promise, and practice in responding to the challenging ethical issues of our time. First, it presents a convincing vision of reality, including the ongoing relationship of the God and the world, that is rooted in our interpretations of scripture, ordinary and mystical experiences, rational reflection on theological affirmations, the presence and witness to God in the Christian tradition and in humankind's noblest spiritual aspirations, and the ever-growing body of knowledge and insight from culture, most especially science, medicine, literature, and the insights of those outside the church. Second, holistic and life-affirming theology believes that we can chart our lives according to our relative, yet life-orienting theological visions. Emerging process theology asserts that healthy theology is "lived theology" that emerges from and guides our experience and behavior in the celebrations and sorrows of everyday life. Finally, holistic theology inspires practices of faithful prayer and action. Nowhere is the interplay of vision, promise, and practice more important than in life and death ethical situations, where we need a moral and spiritual compass to help us find our way.

Holistic theology gives birth to and is shaped by holistic and life-transforming ethics. Ethics concerns the relationship of contemplation and action, that is, how our values and beliefs find expression in the complexities of decision-making in our households, communities, governance, and planetary life. Just as all persons are, by nature, theologians who seek to understand their lives in times of conflict and suffering, so, too, all persons are ethicists insofar as we constantly make choices between "better" and "worse" in the creative challenges of each moment. Indeed, process theology's affirmation that each moment is a process of self-creation that contributes to the ongoing creation of the universe implies that every moment's emergence is implicitly an ethical decision involving its impact on its own and others' future experiences.

Emerging process ethics asks us to consider: *Will our decisions bring beauty to the universe? Will they contribute to the healing of persons and institutions? Will they increase freedom and creativity or constrict persons' ethical and lifestyle options? Or, will they increase personal anguish and contribute to the destructive culture wars of our times?*

God-centered Ethics. In this chapter, I will reflect on the nature of process ethics in terms of personal, community, and planetary transformation. Emerging process ethics is, first of all, God-centered. Each moment emerges from the lively interplay of events, including God's vision for this moment in time. God's vision involves a network of creative and life-affirming possibilities, appropriate to each moment's context and history. While ethical reflection ultimately involves the widening of interest to embrace the well-being of as many creatures as possible beyond ourselves, ethical reflection always begins in each moment's decision-making process.

As we respond to God's ideals for our life, we answer questions such as: *What type of person am I choosing to become? What values shape my experience? What is the impact of my decision-making on the immediate and long-term future, both for others and form myself? What kind of world do I want to emerge as a result of my decision-making?*

Our response to these holy questions reflects our attentiveness to God's still small voice in our lives, our willingness to reach beyond self-interest to choose for the well-being of future lives, including our own future, and our understanding of each moment as our contribution to the quality of life of our families, communities, and the planet.

God-centered in orientation, emerging process ethics sees ethical decision-making in terms of our concrete response to a concrete and intimate God moving through the lives of concrete and unique persons, wrestling with the challenges of complex, concrete situations. God calls us toward wholeness in each moment through the affirmation of our own and others' experiences. God's aim is toward beauty and complexity of experience, not just for us but for persons across the globe and for unborn generations. Our decisions in response to God's call present God not only with a beautiful or ugly universe, or better or worse communities, but also open or close the door to an array of divine possibilities for the future.

When Mother Teresa of Calcutta describes her mission in terms of doing "something beautiful for God," she is portraying the essence of God-centered ethics from a process perspective. Process ethics is not about submissively following abstract commandments, rules, or social mores, as important as some of these structures may be in character development and social relationships. Rather, process ethics involves the dynamic relationship of God's vision for our lives and the planet, including the wisdom embedded in our religious traditions, as it relates to this precious emerging moment of decision and the evolving future that lies ahead.

In contrast to images of God as the source of moral absolutes, process theology sees God as the ultimate relativist, concretely responding to each moment of experience and its environment in light of God's vision of truth, beauty, and goodness. God has a dream for each moment of your life and provides the energy for you to live out God's dream in your own unique and freely chosen way.

When we think ethically from an emerging process perspective, we always have to consider questions such as: *What kind of world am I giving God? What kind of world am I giving my planetary companions? Am I adding to or diminishing the abundant life God seeks for all creation?*

Clearly these questions can lead to various courses of action in our day to day lives and in dramatic life and death situations. While we will never fully understand the exact nature of God's call or the impact of our contribution to God's life, we can always aspire toward actions that bring beauty of experience to as many as possible of our human and non-human companions, knowing that everything we do brings joy or sorrow to God's experience and to the well-being of the planet.

The Ethics of Global Experience. One of the greatest contributions of process theology to ethical reflection is its recognition that ethical consideration applies to non-humans as well as humanity. According to process theology, experience is universal in extent and variable in complexity. Just as God is present as the primary source of order and novelty in every moment of experience, both

143

human and non-human, value pertains to every level of experience, from molecular to human. While universality of experience does not imply consciousness or equality of value, process theology's affirmation that all actual entities are centers experience challenges us to look beyond our species to the well-being of all creation. This is evident in the lively and interdependent creation described in Romans 8 and Psalm 150. The words of Romans 8 proclaim the interconnectedness of human and non-human destiny. Creation groans in its quest for wholeness and beauty of experience. The groaning of creation is reflected in our own inner quest for wholeness, inspired by the Holy Spirit's "sighs too deep for words." Further, if everything can praise God, then each creature deserves our ethical consideration. (Psalm 150:6) When we are truly whole, our wholeness contributes to the well-being of the non-human world and the planet.

God-centered ethics is, by definition, creation-centered ethics. Reverence for creation is fundamental to ethical decision-making insofar as it calls us to be attentive to the immediate and long-term consequences of our actions on spotted owls, polar bears, penguins, fireflies, and polar ice caps, as well as vulnerable fetuses, elder adults, working parents, children, and persons from other lands.

The aim of life, Whitehead asserts, is not only for all creatures, including humans, to live, but for all creatures insofar as it is possible to live well and live better in the context of their ecological niche.[34]   Creaturely experience, however limited in complexity, creativity, or sentience, demands our care and ethical consideration. Nevertheless, our ethical decisions are often a matter of life and death for ourselves, non-humans, and future generations. As Whitehead notes, "life is robbery," that is, our survival depends on the destruction of others, whether animal, vegetable, mineral, or other humans. But, as Whitehead continues, our destruction of others must be ethically justifiable in terms of its role in the achievement of higher values and levels of experience.[35] We must not do harm to other creatures unnecessarily or frivolously. Reverence for life in all its variety and complexity of experience compels us to ask: *Do our necessary, but destructive, choices create more beauty or less beauty for ourselves and the overall community and planet? Is the cost of certain behaviors worthy of the pain that other creatures experience? Are there ways we can live well with minimal ecological destruction and creaturely pain?*

From a process perspective, neither humans, nor animals or fetuses, have absolute moral rights. Guided by our intuition of God's vision of beauty and shalom and the best ethical reflection of our religious traditions, ethical reflection is always related to the interplay of complexity of experience and the concrete situation in which decisions are made. Accordingly, holistic ethical reflection is grounded in the quest for spiritual stature and

---

[34] Alfred North Whitehead, *Function of Reason*, 8.

[35] Alfred North Whitehead, *Process and Reality*, 105.

sensitivity, which enables us to evaluate the circumstances and possible consequences of actions, honor diversity of experience, and look beyond our own self or national interests.

The ethics of global experience (also known as "pan-experientialism" or "panpsychism" among certain process theologians and philosophers) challenges us to recognize the value of each member involved in the process of ethical decision-making. For example, in the case of abortion, emerging process ethics affirms the complex and interdependent moral claims of mothers, fetuses, and significant others involved in the possible termination or continuation of any pregnancy. Emerging process ethics affirms the significance, centrality, and value of pregnant women as the primary ethical decision-makers, with definite rights and responsibilities related to their pregnancy. Concrete complexity of experience and the intimate relationship between a woman and the fetus make the woman's spiritual, economic, and physical well-being primary, at least in the early stages of pregnancy and if the woman's well-being is at significant risk. While fetuses have inherent value from the moment conception, their comparative value in ethical decision-making grows more compelling as they reach more complex levels of experience. The inherent value of fetuses requires that abortion be justified only by compelling personal or social needs. Beyond the ethical significance of women and fetuses are the comparative, but quite relative rights, of spouses, partners, parents, and society as a whole. Reverence for life is essential to process ethics, but the concrete application of reverence for life must be worked out existentially, relationally, and contextually. While we may resist saying that fetal value increases with current or future complexity of experience, this is the safest criteria to employ amid the competing claims of fetus, mother, and culture. Still, at every stage, the fetus deserves moral consideration, both as an experiencing being and in terms of her or his potential as a member of the human community.

Reverence for life, characteristic of process ethics, is consistent with a relational understanding of the current affirmation in the United States of America of *Roe vs. Wade.* Process ethics is committed to reducing the number of abortions to a horizon nearing zero through contraception, including Plan B; values-based sex education, focusing on choice, creativity, abstinence, and responsibility as well as information about contraceptives; and the availability universal health care for every season of life. Process theologians also recognize that reducing the number of abortions is intimately related to issues of economic justice, education and opportunity, gender equality, availability of adoption, and the cultivation of a truly just social order.

I must admit that connecting value, ethical consideration, and complexity of experience is helpful, but also challenging for emerging process ethicists insofar as it suggests the possibility that comparative value decreases as complexity of experience decreases, thus opening the door for involuntary euthanasia, rightly opposed by process theologians and ethicists. In the case of euthanasia, beyond the current complexity of experience are two other criteria of value that must be

147

considered in every ethical decision: the value inherent in a lifetime of experiences and memories and the value of being a beloved child of God, regardless of one's life situation.

At the descending edges of life, while emerging process theology affirms our obligation to care for the most vulnerable members of our communities, persons' fidelity to God and sense of personal vocation may lead them to choose to shorten or end their lives in the context of terminal, chronic, progressive, and debilitating illnesses. In seeking best possibility for our lives in a particular season of life, God's vision of wholeness may embrace the voluntary choice of death as a way of minimizing personal suffering and decreasing the social and economic costs of certain illnesses; it may also involve – and this is the most likely scenario – the choice to withdraw certain life-extending treatments. The God who seeks wholeness in each moment of experience may invite us to ponder the cessation of treatment in order to achieve a sense of personal peace and wholeness amid unrelenting pain or debilitation. Yet, as in the case of abortion, voluntary euthanasia or physician-aided death, must involve the affirmation of God's love for dying persons and, as a matter of personal faith, the recognition that while death is real, it also provides the transition to a new adventure in partnership with God. Still, any premature voluntary ending of a person's life must be evaluated in terms of complexity experience and universality of value as well as the essential reverence of life.

Process theology's reverence for life is reflected in its opposition to involuntary or forced euthanasia of our most vulnerable human companions. Their history of experiences renders them deserving of ethical consideration, despite the lack or diminishing of conscious experience. At a deeper level, our unconscious history and experience continues, even when we can no longer consciously interact with our environment. God does not abandon us even when the ravages of Alzheimer's disease cause us to forget our own identity.

Ethics as contextual and relational. Process theology affirms the universality and variability of revelation, experience, and value. While there are no absolute guidelines, value and reverence are always concrete and contextual in ethical decision-making. Concrete and personal in its ethical orientation, process ethics seeks to achieve the highest experiential values in the present moment and for the foreseeable future. As the apostle Paul notes, "we see in a mirror dimly." (I Corinthians 13:12) Nevertheless, we can anticipate the consequences of certain actions in the immediate and long-term future of ourselves and generations to come. For example, process-relational ethics asks us to consider the consequences of personal decision making and social policy; such questions may challenge us to sacrifice certain values in the present so that other generations of humans and non-humans may survive. We are challenged to live economically sustainable and ecologically sound lives, in the context of the realities of world hunger and global climate change, so that others might simply live. Relational and contextual ethics call us to lower our impact on the environment through lower birth rates, more effective contraception, simpler life styles, green

149

technologies and new energy sources, and an emphasis on the spiritual and relational values rather than materialism and consumption.

Ethics, public policy, and international relations. Emerging process ethics challenges us to see national sovereignty as relative rather than absolute. Nations, like persons, are called to self-affirmation and self-creativity in light of the overarching importance of planetary well-being. Popular phrases, like "America first," become idolatrous when they are absolutized at the expense of the sovereignty of other nations and care for the earth. In an interdependent and evolving world, there is no room for empire or nationalism, whether American, Chinese, Iranian, Israeli, Palestinian, or Russian. As a living organism, embracing nation-states, human and non-human creatures, sea life, and plant and mineral life, the health of planet earth depends on the dynamic interdependence of each constitutive part. The apostle Paul's image of the body of Christ relates to the relationship of nations, and humans and non-humans, as well as to the health of the church. The morality of nations is judged by a nation's contributions to human creativity and non-human survival.

Process theology promotes negotiation, compromise, and partnership in personal and international affairs. Nations have a right to secure the economic and personal well-being of their citizens and this is best done through the interplay of national self-affirmation and respect for the appropriate sovereignty of other lands. In the body of Christ, which extends beyond the church to embrace the whole earth, the well-being of other lands contributes to our own national well-being. This is especially true in terms of issues of economic well-being, ecology, and human rights. Our quest for economic security and beauty of experience is intimately connected with our affirmation of the same values for citizens of other lands.

In a world characterized by dynamic interdependence, reverence for life includes compassionate and just care for "undocumented workers" or "undocumented residents" in our midst. Our calling is to welcome them as God's beloved children while affirming the well-being of our own citizens. If we come to believe, based on sound economic judgment, that reducing illegal immigration is valuable to our national well-being, process ethics counsels us to support economic and political justice, embodied in fair wages and accessible and good health care, in the lands from which illegal immigrants come as well as in our own land. Process ethics invites us to see the well-being of other lands and the survival of non-human species as essential aspects of any holistic approach to international relations and foreign affairs. God's love embraces and seeks wholeness for all persons and all nations. Process theologians imagine a world in which shalom and prosperity characterize the affairs of every nation and the relationships among the nations of the world.

Living Process
An Emerging Spiritual Practice

Process theology affirms the interplay of vision and action in personal and communal ethics. Ethics begins with a vision of global value (pan-experientialism) and embodies that vision in everyday life.   In this exercise, we begin with a time of quiet breathing, awakening to God's spirit with each breath.   Visualize God's breath as a healing light entering your whole being.   From this personal center, experience God's light embracing your body, mind, and s p i r i t ... t h e n ,   e m b r a c i n g   y o u r family...community...nation....the non-human world in all its variety...and the planet. Visualize the whole planet as being bathed in God's healing light...from that planetary center   return   to   the   non-human   world...   nation... community...family...and your self.

In the interplay of the spirit moving through your self and the world, take some time to reflect on what transforming actions you are called to in light of your vision of the planet and its inhabitants.

Chapter Nine

Emerging Process Spirituality

> Religion is what a person does with his [or her] solitariness...if you are never solitary, you cannot be religious.[36]

VIRTUALLY EVERY MORNING, I TAKE a sunrise walk, which joins prayer and aerobic exercise. After my morning meditation, I leave the house for about forty five minutes, walking through my hilly neighborhood at the edge of Lancaster, PA. I rejoice in the singing of birds, but I also take time to open myself to divine energy from head to toe as I pray for the day ahead and for persons and situations that are important to me. Sometimes, I visualize the persons on my "prayer list"; other times I give persons a distant reiki healing energy treatment; still other times, I simply give thanks for the many blessings

---

[36] Alfred North Whitehead, *Religion in the Making* (New York: Meridian, 1972), 16.

that fill my life.[37]   Throughout my walk, I repeat affirmations related to each aspect of my personal, professional, and relational life. I return home looking forward to a strong cup of coffee and the adventures of the day ahead. My morning spiritual practices integrate the solitude of personal prayer and meditation with the interdependence and communal orientation of intercessory prayer.

Today, many persons describe their personal journeys by the phrase, "I'm spiritual but not religious." They believe that spirituality involves our lively personal relationship with the holy, while religion relates to moribund creeds, rules, and congregations. In response to such critiques, emerging process theology provides pathways to holiness that embrace the intimate spontaneity of spiritual experience with the life-transforming traditions and institutional activities of vital religious communities. Emerging process theology seeks to join tradition and novelty in such a way that persons can affirm that they are both spiritual and religious.

For emerging process theology, spirituality is both individual and social in nature. While we need time for quiet contemplation, emerging process spirituality affirms that we can't be spiritual without profoundly immersing ourselves in our relationships, both interpersonal and institutional, and with the ambient and mysterious universe. We are all part of the intricate and dynamic body of Christ, radiating from our own spiritual centers

---

[37] For more on reiki healing, see Bruce Epperly and Katherine Epperly, *Reiki Healing Touch and the Way of Jesus* (Kelowna, British Columbia: 2005.

to embrace the whole universe. Spiritual practices enable us to experience God's presence in the multi-faceted ecology from which our lives emerge each moment of the day. Still, spirituality also involves our own creative self-centering in relationship with a dynamic ever-changing and evolving God.

At the heart of emerging process spirituality is the affirmation that God is present as a source of guidance and inspiration in every moment of experience and in every encounter. According to process theology, all things and every moment reveal the holy. Accordingly, spiritual formation involves the intentional and ongoing process of deepening our experience God in the ordinary and extraordinary moments of life. With the Benedictine monastic tradition, process theologians find God's presence in greeting a stranger, taking care of tools, logging on to your computer, answering the telephone, making an update on Facebook, and checking your e-mail. God is everywhere and in every thing. Put personally, this means that you are also a revelation of God, and so is your neighbor! God inspires each moment of your life, for you and all things, "live and move and have your being in God."

God is in this Place. The Hebraic scriptures tell the story of Jacob's encounter with divine. (Genesis 28:10-17) One night, Jacob dreamed of a ladder in which angels ascended and descended, moving from heaven to earth and back to heaven again. Jacob awakens from his dream and exclaims, "God was in this place – and I did not know it." Jacob's dream is a model for our own religious journeys: spirituality enables us to encounter God in this and every

155

place, so that we can exclaim, "God is in this place and now I know it." Every place can be the gate of heaven for those who awaken to God's ever-present companionship.

As we look at the story of Jacob's dream, it is interesting to note that the angels were, first, ascending and, then, descending. Revelation is not other-worldly, nor does it draw us away from the complexities this world. It arises from our concrete experience of God's wholeness/holiness in the here and now of historic, relational, and embodied experiences. Encountering God calls us to love God in this concrete, ever-emerging world, rather than deferring issues of justice, peace, and self-realization to a disembodied afterlife.

The Celtic tradition speaks of "thin places," in which the God energetically reveals Godself in ordinary life – in stone circles, woodlands, and unexpected encounters with humans and non-human companions. In that same spirit, process theology affirms that all places can become "thin places" through which God encounters us in our own flesh and blood encounters, transforming, deepening, and widening our experience.

Emerging process spirituality immerses us in the world and in the body. Many forms of spirituality deny the importance of embodiment. These spiritualities see the body as a "prison house," filled with desires that take us away from God. In contrast, emerging process spirituality invites us to see God in the very cells of our bodies: the heavens declare the glory of God and so do our immune, pulmonary, reproductive, and circulatory systems. Our basic human desires for companionship, sexuality and sustenance reveal God's presence. With the apostle Paul, process theology proclaims that our bodies are the "temple of God." Healthy spirituality enables us to "glorify God" in our embodiment through acts of loving connection. Truly the body is inspired and the spirit embodied.

Wonderful Spirituality. Rabbi Abraham Joshua Heschel affirmed that authentic religious experience is grounded in the experience of "radical amazement." Spiritual formation enables us to experience the wonder of each moment and every task. God reveals Godself as the deepest reality of each moment of experience. A wonderful spirituality reminds us, in the spirit of songwriter Peter Mayer, that we live in the holy here and now, in which all things can be experienced as holy now.[38]

Process theology asserts that reality is dynamic as well as relational. Accordingly, spirituality involves immersion in, rather than escape from, the flux of life. As the source of creative transformation and cosmic evolution, God's revelation to us is also constantly changing. Although God is ever-faithful and constant in love for creation, God's presence in our lives – God's call to wholeness and beauty – changes, albeit incrementally, from moment to moment. God's love is new every morning. Spiritual transformation involves immersing ourselves in the constantly changing, shape-shifting movements of God in our lives and in the world. "God is still speaking" and we are most attuned to God when we embrace new and creative images of God and ourselves.

---

[38] Peter Mayer, "Holy Now"

God is also still touching, listening, feeling, tasting, and smelling. Spiritual growth awakens us to new and creative multi-sensory encounters with God – relationally, vocationally, institutionally, and politically.

God's creativity calls us to be God's creative companions in healing and bringing beauty to the earth. We are not meant to be passive in our acceptance of what some people define as God's will for us. Rather, we are challenged to do something new and beautiful for God. We are called to bring something new into the world that would have not occurred apart from the embodiment of our spiritual commitments in daily life. Spirituality involves adventure, not mere repetition. Practiced regularly, rituals ground us in the here and now, but rituals also set us free to follow unexpected pathways to adventure. In the context of an emerging universe, emerging process theology asserts that God likes surprises, too! We are most faithful to God when we color outside the lines, giving God a world that even God had not fully anticipated.

Pathways of the Spirit. There are many paths to consciously experience the divine. Process theology affirms that, at the deepest level, we all experience God. Process theology invites us to create various forms of "Christian yoga" or pathways of the Spirit to respond to the experiences and gifts of different personality types, age groups, ethnicities, and religious and liturgical styles. No one spiritual practice fits all persons, personality types, or seasons of life. Lively spirituality is multi-dimensional, protean, and intimate in its reflection of God's own lively and protean creativity.

Spiritual practices such as prayer and meditation awaken us to God's intimate presence and enable God to be present in our lives in new and surprising ways. We can also pray with our hands in service and in healing touch as well as with words and sacraments. Imaginative prayers (*lectio divina* and Ignatian spirituality) awaken us to God's ever-expanding revelation in our lives. The many-faceted Christian practices bring to consciousness the ever-present divinity whose constant and intimate inspiration is often overlooked in the busyness of everyday of life.

In our spiritual lives, we are called to be innovative, and to employ ancient spiritual practices in new ways. As Christians, we can creatively integrate global healing practices in our own spiritual journeys. Zen Buddhist meditation, Hindu yoga, Islamic/Sufi dance, Native American chanting, and Asian reiki healing touch can awaken and deepen our experience of the Living God, and be joined with traditionally Christian prayers and meditation. In a constantly changing world, we are most faithful to God's constantly emerging revelation when we adapt Christian and global practices to respond creatively to our particular time and place. Each practice opens us to a new vision of God and a new way to walk the pathways of the Spirit.

Living Process
An Emerging Spiritual Practice

Process theology's vision of an omnipresent and omni-active God invites you to listen to your life. While there are many pathways of the spirit, process spirituality invites us to listen to the deeper voices of God within and amid all the other voices. I use the word "voices" here because process theology recognizes that God presents each person with many voices and possibilities, rather than just one ideal vision, for each moment of experience and community. Here are a number of pathways to living process theology:

First, take time regularly to listen to your dreams, to hunches, intuitions, synchronous moments. God is still speaking in each and every moment of life. Spiritual guide Gerald May captures the essence of process spirituality in terms of the interplay of pausing, noticing, opening, stretching and yielding.[39] Process theology sees responding to God's call as the final step in our emerging spiritual experiences. We listen and see, and then respond with actions that honor our experience of God in all things. Our responses open up new pathways for divine and human creativity.[40]

Second, process theology invites us to look deeply at the persons with whom we daily interact. If God is new every

---

[39] See Gerald May, *The Awakened Heart* (New York: Harper Collins, 1993).

40

For more on this approach, see Bruce and Katherine Epperly, *Tending to the Holy: The Practice of the Presence of God in Ministry* (Herndon, VA: Alban Institute, 2009).

morning, then God's novelty calls us to novel ways of seeing and acting. We can greet each day with a "beginner's mind." We can commit ourselves to seeing God speak to you through every encounter! We can see God within and beneath our lives and actions. Each day we can make a commitment to experience God as the deepest realities of ourselves and those whom we meet. We can receive revelations in moments of quiet but also in our interactions with store clerks and family members. God speaks through all things, inspiring us in every encounter.

Third, God invites you to claim your own identity as a revelation of divine love. Breathe deeply. Experience God breathing through you! God's presence is also your deepest and highest reality. Claim your own identity as God's beloved son or daughter.

Fourth, emerging process theology invite you to see each day as a holy adventure. One of my spiritual practices as I begin each day is to whisper to myself the words of Psalmist, "This is the day that God has made. I will rejoice and be glad in it!" Then, I ask "What great thing will be asked of me? What new adventure will I be called to share in?" In this way, I begin the day adventurously, embarking with God as my companion on a holy adventure.

Chapter Ten

Process-Relational Evangelism

I am confident of this, that the one who
began a good work among you will bring it
to completion by the day of Jesus Christ.[41]

IN THE EARLY SEVENTIES, MY BEST FRIEND Wendy and I
went to what we thought was renaissance faire in
Riverside, California. Unbeknownst to us, the faire was
sponsored by a Christian outreach ministry. When one of
the "knights" invited me to have a talk about spirituality
in his room, I accepted, unaware that he would corner me
and then pepper me with scriptures until I let him pray
the "sinner's prayer" with me just to get out of the room!
When I was finally released from his evangelistic clutches,
I felt manipulated and violated by his hard sell and
unilateral approach to sharing the good news of Jesus
Christ.

Many progressive Christians wonder if evangelism
can truly be "good news" for spiritual seekers. Just
mention evangelism to a group of progressive Christians
and the response will be as positive as the latest political

---

[41] Philippians 1:5

initiative by the "religious right." Many progressive Christians have experienced the theological or spiritual trauma of growing up in conservative congregations or encountering confident apostles of Jesus who make it clear that anyone who fails to agree with their pathway to salvation is doomed to an eternity of hell-fire and brimstone. To most progressive Christians, the majority of evangelistic techniques rely on manipulation, pressure, dishonesty, and threat.

Many persons have experienced evangelism as a form of violence. In the words of one of my mentors, Bernard Loomer, most evangelistic techniques reflect a unilateral understanding of power, in which persons are told that the only way that they can find personal fulfillment and salvation is to follow a certain way of understanding God, repeat distinctive theological language, and attend select bible-believing churches. Many approaches to evangelism imply that in order to be saved, persons have to give up what is most precious in their current personal lives or in their culture's traditions in order to follow "the way, the truth, and the life" as articulated specifically by the one witnessing to you.

By definition, such ways of evangelism are violent, precisely because they are one-sided in approach, preaching but not listening, giving but not receiving, insisting on the truth of their position while being equally certain that they have nothing of importance to learn from others. While claiming to share the love of Christ, their love is conditional: you are accepted by God and by God's ambassadors if, and only if, you adopt their way of life and their approach to God.

Progressive Christians are right in opposing violent and unilateral methods of evangelism and the theology that undergirds them. Nevertheless, spiritual and theological vitality are nurtured and inspired by what we affirm about God and not what we disbelieve and deny in matters of faith.

I believe that emerging process theology has good news to share. This book is dedicated to the spirit-rejuvenating, life-transforming, and world-shaping, vision of emerging process theology. With the future of our churches and the world at stake, our calling is to share good news in ways that heal, transform, and reconcile persons in our postmodern, pluralistic age.

Emerging process theology suggests both a vision and a practice for today's "progressive evangelists." First, process theology sees evangelism as relational and non-violent in nature. In line with the interdependence of life, evangelism is always personal, contextual, and communal. We share God's good news with persons in ways that speak to their unique cultural, spiritual, and relational situation. Holistic evangelism listens as well as shares in response to the experiences of unique persons whom we encounter.

Second, emerging process theology recognizes that God is already at work in the lives of those with whom we share God's good news. This is the practical implication of the Christian understanding omnipresence. God is truly present in inspiring and healing ways in every life and every situation. Further, as John's gospel asserts, "the true light enlightens everyone." In his own evangelistic sermon at the Areopagus in Athens, the apostle Paul witnesses to the universality and intimacy of divine revelation and the God in whom "we live and move and have our being." What makes the Paul's comment more significant for a theology of evangelism is that Paul correctly attributes this often-quoted "Christian" scripture to Greek philosophical wisdom. In light of this, process theologians note that when we share our good news with others, God is not only inspiring our words and deeds but also the words and deeds of those to whom we witness. Sharing the good news is, by definition, edifying to everyone in the conversation and not just the one with whom we share our faith.

Third, emerging process theology sees evangelism as an opportunity to listen as well as share God's good news. Bernard Loomer captured the spirit of process evangelism with his use of the word "size" as descriptive of healthy spirituality and theological reflection. Spiritual size, or stature, implies, according to Loomer, the depth and breadth of reality that we can embrace without losing our personal center or faith-perspective. If our message lacks "size," it will eventually become irrelevant or destructive to us or others. In sharing our faith with others, we must be open to becoming transformed as a result of our conversations. Progressive Christians need to be willing to grow in their understanding of God's presence in the lives of atheists, agnostics, and persons of other faiths as well as their more conservative Christian brothers and sisters. While progressive Christians seldom enter into serious theological conversations with conservative Christians, we must be open to the wisdom of conservative Christians whose faith is grounded in an emphasis on stability, certainty, and tradition in the life of faith. In hearing others into speech, emerging process evangelists open the door to mutual spiritual transformation and the possibility that our witness may bring a new sense of hope and meaning in the lives of those with whom we share our faith as well as our own lives.

Evangelism embraces both vision and practice. The relational and non-violent practices of emerging process evangelism point to open-spirited, creative, inclusive, and relational visions of God. God inspires and affirms many paths to wholeness, and so should we. With a sense of confidence in the lively and emerging faith we affirm, process theologians can share the good news reflected in the following life-transforming and mission-oriented affirmations of faith. These affirmations open both giver and receiver, and speaker and listener, to new experiences of God, who is present in the lives of those to whom we share the good news of God's grace. Take a moment to reflect on these "good news" affirmations:

God lovingly seeks to heal every person and all creation. All persons are welcome in God's loving community. Evangelism proclaims that God loves you, that your life matters to God, and that God wants us to find wholeness and joy.

God is present in your life right now, inspiring you to grow personally and spiritually. With God working quietly, yet tirelessly, in your life, you can become free of the past and open to God's future. Within every "dead end," there are new possibilities for spiritual growth and personal transformation. If you listen, you will

167

experience God's ongoing visions for your life and the world around you.

God wants you to experience freedom and creativity in your life. God invites you to become a partner in creating the world today and the world to come. God rejoices in surprise, creativity, and beauty, and invites us to rejoice in these as well. In an unfinished world, your life can truly make a difference.

God never gives up on anyone or anything. From the wreckage of our lives, God seeks to bring forth something of beauty. Regardless of the past, God will not abandon us, but will find new and creative ways to awaken us to holy relationships with God and all creation.

There is hope in every situation because divine possibility abounds. Even when there can't be a physical cure or we must live with the realities of trauma, addiction, or chronic illness, we can experience God's healing presence that allows us to live with faith and courage in the most difficult situations.

Your life makes a difference to God and can be the tipping point between life and death for your community and the planet. God's embrace of the world is a "tender care that nothing be lost." [42] Our openness to God's vision for our lives and the world creates new possibilities for personal and global transformation. Like the young boy with the five loaves and two fish, what we perceive to be our meager gifts can provide a meal large enough to feed a multitude.

From beginning to end, we are embraced by God's everlasting love. Truly nothing can separate us from the love of God. All things dwell in God's everlasting love. This beloved world calls us to acts of love, kindness, and

---

[42] Alfred North Whitehead, *Process and Reality,* 346

transformation. But, beyond this life-time, God calls each of us to share in a holy adventure, in which creativity stretches onward to infinity. We do not know what we shall become, but God's dreams for our future are always more than we can imagine.

Freed from threat and exclusivity, process evangelism welcomes, nurtures, and edifies seekers and believers as companions in healing the earth.

Living Process
An Emerging Spiritual Practice

Holistic evangelism arises from our experience of God's movements in our lives. Our sharing God's "good news" with others begins with our recognition of the God-moments in our own lives as well as in the non-Christian world. Accordingly, the practice of spiritual autobiography undergirds healthy evangelism. Listening to our lives as a prelude for sharing the good news is undergirded by questions such as:

- *When did you first experience God's presence in your life?*
- *What religious challenges have you experienced? What are your most significant questions of faith?*
- *What is your current image of God? How has your image of God evolved over the years?*
- *What gives your life meaning?*

169

- *Where have you felt God's presence most fully in your church? When did you feel most alive in worship or service?*
- *In what ways have you encountered persons from other faith traditions or no faith tradition? How have these encounters shaped your understanding of God?*
- *If you had only one thing you could share about the way of Jesus, what would it be?*
- *If you had only thing to share about the gifts of my congregation, what would it be?*

Chapter Eleven

Salvation and Wholeness

Nothing in all creation will be able to
separate us from the love   o f G o d i n
Christ Jesus our [Healer].[43]

RECENTLY A DEAR FRIEND TOLD ME of a dream she had
during a time of personal and spiritual transition. In the
course of her dream, she heard God tell her that she no
longer loved her because she was questioning her long-
held spiritual path.

Kate had a similar encounter with a parishioner
following the death of her daughter as a result of an
overdose of sleeping pills. Her parishioner asked, with
tears in her eyes, "Where is Susie now?" She was
concerned that because of her suicide, Susie would spend
eternity in hell.

Throughout this book we have asserted that
emerging process theology sees inspiration and revelation
as both universal and personal. God works to bring
wholeness in every situation. But, God's passion for
wholeness, beauty, and justice is always concrete,

---

[43] Romans 8:39

contextual, and shaped by the many factors from which each moment of experience emerges. Our lives are an ongoing creative synthesis involving the interplay of God's call and our response in the context of the impact of factors such as the environment, our past decisions, overall health, economics, ethnicity, and family of origin.

For many Christians, salvation is a static event, something we have to await upon until we die. These Christians believe that there is an unbridgeable chasm between this life and the next. To such Christians, this lifetime is the "front porch" to eternity. They believe that our true goal is heaven, while earth is merely a preparation for the life to come. From this perspective, the God who seeks to save us in this life gives up on us at the moment of death and the meaning of this life is reduced to our relationship with Jesus, usually articulated in propositional or doctrinal rather than ethical terms. These Christians also see the pathway to salvation as clear and distinct – whether in terms of doctrine, participation in the sacraments, individualistic ethics, or relationship with Jesus. They believe that God is limited, or limits Godself, in the ways God can bring wholeness and salvation to human beings. Indeed, for some Christians, a propositional relationship with Jesus, involving saying the right doctrinal words, is the only way to encounter God in this life and the next.

In contrast, emerging process theology sees life as a whole and holy adventure, embracing this moment and all the adventures to come. While process theologians do not emphasize heaven, or the afterlife, as the sole focus of the spiritual journey, they see continuity between earth and heaven, this life and the next. Our experiences and actions in this life contribute to the quality of our lives beyond the grave. In this way, process theology avoids the Marxist critique of religion as an "opiate" that turns persons' attention from the challenges of injustice and oppression in this lifetime toward a heavenly home in which all of our problems will be solved and this life will fall into insignificance. Emerging process theology affirms that what we do in this life matters eternally both to God and in the ongoing history of the universe. What we do and how we live our lives also contributes to the eternal journey of our fellow beings.

While progressive in spirit, process thought takes the traditional image of resurrection seriously, although not literally. The resurrection of the person affirms that any post-mortem state we can imagine embraces, transforms, and heals our earthly life. We do not "lose something" in the afterlife, rather what dies in terms of physical embodiment is raised as spiritual in the most holistic sense of the word. (I Corinthians 15) Further, process theology, in the spirit of the biblical images of the body of Christ and shalom, sees post-mortem existence as communal rather than individualistic in nature.

Although process theology affirms that salvation is universal, the fullness of salvation, or growth beyond the grave, is not automatic. Rather, the same creativity and freedom that exist in the earthly sphere will also exist beyond the grave. Personal identity, beyond the grave, means that our current lives are not lost, but will continue in a process of ongoing creative transformation beyond the grave. We will grow and evolve, forgiving and being forgiven, coming to terms with our past earthly life, as our spirits expand to embrace God's passion for our lives. The afterlife is a time for growth, transformation, and enlightenment in a realm in which our quest for wholeness-in-community is unambiguously supported. God's aim at healing in this life is carried out in the next life, but without environmental hindrance or impediment. God's attitude toward us does not change at the hour of our deaths. God will continue to call and we will continue to respond in our own unique ways in our adventures beyond this lifetime.

"If all are saved, what good is Christ? Does belief make a difference" asks the conservative Christian. "Don't we need the threat of hell to bring persons to Christ or encourage moral behavior?"

Emerging process theology responds to these questions with both a "yes" and a "no." Belief matters insofar as healthy beliefs shape our openness to God and transformation in this lifetime, which will have an impact on the quality of life after death. But, we come to experience God's relationship to us ultimately through love and not fear. "Hell" symbolically points to an essential element in the justice of life and the impact of our actions in bringing us closer or turning us further away from God's vision of our lives. Our acts in this lifetime have consequences and shape our post-mortem experience and the afterlives of others.

Yes, belief in Christ has everlasting importance. Christ, embodied in Jesus the healer, inspires our commitment to wholeness in this life and the next not only for ourselves but for all creation. Our attitude toward Christ matters. In awakening to Christ's loving presence, we become open to God's passion for our lives in this world. As the Eastern Church affirms, "God became human so that humans might become divine." Christ is alive, and inspires us to have the "mind of Christ" in all that we do.

In contrast to the dualism of saved and unsaved and heaven and hell, emerging process theology asserts that faith is not a rescue operation, but involves our evolving openness to larger dimensions of reality. We believe in God not to escape hell, but to experience God's love in this lifetime and share this love with others. Indeed, experiencing God may challenge us to reject the norms of our culture, even those held by persons of faith, in order to follow God's passion for our lives.

At a preaching retreat I attended at Kirkridge Retreat Center in Poconos of Pennsylvania, nearly twenty-five years ago, I recall hearing noted preacher Ernie Campbell assert that, "there are only two kinds of persons in the world – those who are in God's hands and know it; and those who are in God's hands and don't know it." Faith opens us to awareness of God's eternal care and presence in our lives. Faith also opens us to embrace God's power in our lives and in the transformation of the world. Indeed, if God is actively present everywhere, every place is "heavenly" and every place is "home." Faith helps us discover God's nearness in all things, including our own experience. Further, if we see our lifetime in terms of a holy adventure which extends beyond the grave, then we can take risks for justice and transformation, knowing that we will always receive second chances to more fully experience God's dream of abundant life for ourselves and the planet. If we trust God's presence as the giver of everlasting life, then we can live with the confidence that "nothing can separate us from the love of God in Christ Jesus our Lord." (Romans 8:39)

Do we know what the afterlife is really like? Will we have relationships beyond the grave? What shall we hope for in terms of our concrete experiences beyond the grave?

While process theology has been humble in terms of describing the afterlife, I believe that God is equally present in this world and the next, although the impediments to knowing God may be overcome in our adventures beyond the grave. In the "heavenly realm," we can grow in spirit and relatedness without fear, defensiveness, or obstruction. Beyond the grave, the holy adventure that characterized this lifetime continues and expands to creatively embrace our partners in a never-ending journey.

Process theology sees all of life, both this life and the next, as dynamic, evolving, and interdependent. If this lifetime tells us something about the afterlife, then we can expect to have relationships beyond the grave. Perhaps, we will continue to grow, within a healing and nurturing environment, with those with whom we were closest in this life. Perhaps, we will also "leave home" to encounter those who have inspired us by their actions, words, and writing. We may meet new friends and mentors who will inspire our growth and grow along with us in the afterlife.

Neither human beings nor the cosmos is ever complete. Our postmodern, pluralistic adventure involves growth in stature – the self expands to embrace the whole, and to experience its own wholeness and well-being as connected with the well-being of all things. Salvation embraces all things in a continuing adventure that will eventually include all creation, both human and non-human. In our ever-evolving cosmos, God truly will be all in all!

Living Process
An Emerging Spiritual Practice

Visions of the afterlife call us to imaginative prayer. In this spiritual practice, we will explore our vision of the afterlife and the relationship of this lifetime and the next from a process perspective.

Take a few moments to center your spirit by breathing with God's Spirit. In the stillness, imagine yourself taking a long journey with God as your companion. As you take your final earthly breaths, imagine God or Jesus leading you to a new adventure in holy companionship. What do you first notice beyond the grave? What is your environment like? Do you notice any familiar persons? What type of "body" do you have?

As you become acclimated to the next steps of your spiritual journey, your holy companion asks you the following question, "What adventures do you wish to have now?

Where would you like to grow in your life?" Take some time to explore your vision of future growth.

As you continue to converse with your holy companion, your companion asks, "What were your most joyous moments on earth? What moments would you like to take with you? Who were your spiritual companions on earth?" Take time to visualize these moments and persons, giving thanks for the wonders of this earthly lifetime.

As the dialogue continues, your holy companion asks you to review your life. Your companion lovingly asks, "What was your greatest regret of your earthly life? What do you wish that you had done in your earthly lifetime?" Without judgment or guilt, take a few minutes to review any regrets or tasks left undone.

Continuing your journey with your holy companion, you notice the beauty of the world in which you find yourself as you remember the beauty of life on earth. Take time to give thanks to the God of heaven and earth and life and death.

As you conclude, ponder those persons who were your spiritual companions, whether spouses, partners, or spiritual friends. Make a commitment to deepen your love for them in this lifetime. Think a moment about regrets and tasks undone. Ask God to guide and energize you to live a life of beauty, love, and action, a life of holy partnership with God and your earthly companions. Ask God to guide you in recognizing your vocation – and vocations – in this lifetime.

Conclusion

A Never Ending Adventure

For now we see in a mirror dimly, but then we will see face to face. Now, I know only in part; then I will know fully, even as I have been fully known.

And now faith, hope, and love abide, these three, and the greatest of these is love.[44]

EMERGING PROCESS THEOLOGY PROCLAIMS that theology is a creative process, in which we are constantly growing in experience, understanding, and wisdom. Theology, like creation itself, is an unending and evolving adventure, in which the present moment emerges from the energy of all that has preceded it and leans toward a surprising and unknown future. Theology, accordingly, is always tentative and subject to transformation and growth. New images of God and humankind emerge in the interplay of divine call, human response, and the ongoing social and planetary advance.

---

[44] I Corinthians 13:12-13

Throughout this book, we have highlighted the dynamic and creative nature of life as it evolves on the personal and cosmic levels. The Living God who brought forth order and novelty in the first moments of creation, nearly fourteen billion years ago, is still bringing forth galaxy upon galaxy. God is still speaking, and creation is still emerging, whether in the evolving human adventure or in the challenging future of planet earth. God's aim is toward wholeness moment by moment even as God imagines possibilities for our distant planetary horizon. While God is an infinite wellspring of possibilities, even God cannot fully know or exactly determine the future that lies ahead. The openness of the future may fill us, in this time of international, economic, and ecological uncertainly, with fear and trembling, but it may also call us to become creative adventurers in companionship with God who seeks to heal the earth.

Emerging process theology asserts that the future remains open for God and for us. The future is also open for the evolution of process theology itself. Theology is a creative adventure in which new insights serve to inspire further insights. Process theology, and progressive Christianity, are constantly emerging, embracing the wisdom of the past, rejoicing in the creativity of the present, and living expectantly toward the novelty of God's future. Awakening to God's vision in our time involves originating novelty to match the novelties of the world in which we live. The novelty that calls us to innovation pertains to theological reflection as well as to our role as God's partners in responding to our current international, congregational, and planetary crises.

Process theology must be willing to embrace new visions and practices if it is to remain attuned with God's evolving universe.[45]

If process theology is to continue inspire current and future generations of progressive, mainline, and open and relational evangelicals as well as seekers and pilgrims, it must actively and intentionally originate novel theological visions and spiritual practices to match the novelties of the world. First, process theology must let go of its identification with the modern and enlightenment world views. Many process and progressive theologians have often been too "conservative" in their response to mysticism, healing, paranormal experiences, and images of survival after death. The adventurous God envisaged by emerging process theology invites us to look beyond sight and sense in order to entertain imaginative images of religious experience, mysticism, and survival after death. In an emerging universe, there is always more to life than we imagine. We can awaken to mystical experiences and live hopefully in this lifetime as we anticipate further growth beyond this lifetime while affirming the goodness of this life and this earth and our responsibility as God's partners in healing the planet. We can be agnostic about the nature of personal journeys beyond the grave, while

---

[45]

Philip Clayton's *Transforming Christian Theology* (Minneapolis: Fortress, 2009) and the Center for Process Studies Transforming Theology program is an important step in this direction www.transformingtheology.org

constructively exploring near death experiences and cross-cultural images of everlasting life.

Second, emerging process theologians need to create progressive spiritual practices to match the novelty of our current religious situation. Theology finds its meaning in the interplay of vision and practice and, today, our visions and practices must encompass the pluralism in Christianity and other world religions. We must go beyond our liberal biases, and embrace the vitality of Pentecostal and evangelical as well as Buddhist, Hindu, African, and First American spiritual practices. The vocation of emerging process theology will be found in "living" process theology rather than merely thinking about it!

Third, emerging process Christians need to embrace many voices and media in worship. Fidelity to God's Spirit in a pluralistic age inspires us to embrace the many varieties of communal spiritual experience. In the course of worship, we may experience Christ's healing and transforming presence in Celtic poetry, Navajo chants, African rhythms, Hispanic melodies, and Euro-American cadences. We may dance, contemplate, share in healing touch, and explore imaginative visions. Centered in Christ, our many voices join in one great chorus of creative transformation.

Finally, the adventure is emerging in ways that we cannot fully imagine. But, despite our concerns about the survival of mainstream and progressive Christianity, emerging process theologians are inspired to live by a hopeful and open future: to embody theology in practices that heal the earth and to share our theological and spiritual vision in the spiritual marketplace as a clear and convincing alternative to conservative evangelical Christianity, the religious right, and new age spiritualities.

As the wellspring of hopeful possibilities, God is alive and moving in our lives and in the universe. We can share our good news with seekers, bring healing to vulnerable persons, grow new and innovative congregations, work to bring justice to our communities, and explore innovative ways to save the good earth, because God's future is open and emerging in unexpected and hopeful ways. Remember the fireflies! Life is emerging and new possibilities bursting forth. Look to the growing edge!

Living Process
An Emerging Spiritual Practice

In this exercise, take time to imagine contemplatively your personal future. What dreams is God calling you toward? What holy relationships lie on the horizon?

Now, look at the future of progressive Christianity and process theology. What images of growth do you see for the Christianity of the future? Finally, as you look at the planet's future, in all its uncertainty, what hopes do you have for the future? What visions of planetary healing can you imagine? Take time to experience imaginatively your positive visions of the future.

Conclude by inviting God to give you more lively and creative images of the future and to give you hope and energy for transforming the world and your own life. Then, invite God to give you insights in terms of what you might actively do to bring about the first fruits of God's shalom on earth.

Bruce G. Epperly

Emerging Questions for Conversation and Group Study

Introduction and Chapter One

If you are studying in a group setting, begin each session with an "emerging spiritual practice" either found in the appropriate chapter or in the study guide itself. Let your study be whole person, inviting each member to experience emerging process thought spiritually, relationally, and emotionally, as well as intellectually. In the spirit of process though, honor diverse voices as differing and often complementary pathways to a larger truth. Remember the importance of perspective as a way of honoring personal experience as well as deepening the experience of a community or group.

As you begin this first study, take time to share your hopes for the class. Then, take time to practice breath prayer: quietly and intentionally observe your breathing, inhaling and exhaling as you center yourself in God's presence in your life and in the group.

1) How do you understand the nature of freedom? What is the role of past events in shaping the present? In what ways do we go beyond our past experiences? Can we affirm both personal freedom and the impact of our environment, DNA, and other factors on our moment-by-moment and ongoing experiences?

2) How do you respond to Victor Frankl's affirmation: "everything can be taken away from a [person] but one thing...to choose one's attitude in any given set of

circumstances?" How might this affirmation of freedom, amid limitation, be helpful to a person with a life-threatening illness or who has just lost her or his job or who is suffering from the impact of childhood trauma? How might you find it helpful in your life situation?

3) Reflecting on your understanding of scripture: Do you recognize any emerging process themes within the scriptural witness? Do you notice affirmations within scripture of the significance of relationship, dynamic change, freedom, both in human and divine activity?

4) What does it mean to speak of having a "relationship" with God? What does relationship mean from God's standpoint? And, what does the divine-human relationship mean from our own human standpoint? In what ways, have you experienced God in your life? How have your experiences of the holy transformed your life?

5) Take some time to read and then quietly reflect on the story of Jacob's dream of a ladder of angels (Genesis 28:10-17). What do you make of the angels ascending from earth to heaven? What is your response to Jacob's affirmation, "surely God was in this place – but I did not know it"? As you consider your own spiritual journey, do you have a sacred place – your own Beth-el, or gate of heaven?

6) Do you think non-humans are able to experience the world in creative and sensitive ways? What difference does it make spiritually or ethically, if non-humans are

also centers of experience and can respond to environmental stimuli? Can non-humans have a meaningful relationship with God? If a five year old child were to ask you if his dog were going to heaven, how would you respond?

7) What does it mean to suggest that the universe influences every moment of your experience? Is this good or ambiguous news?

8) If relationship with God and one another is primary in emerging process theology, how do our relationships with God and one another shape our religious practices? How might we balance solitude and relationship in our spiritual lives?

9) If the world is dynamic and evolving, how does the dynamic nature of life shape your current understanding of theological truth and doctrine? Can we act with conviction even if we recognize the limitations of our deeply-held beliefs?

Conclude with a time of silent openness to God's presence in our lives and in the group. Take time once again to breathe deeply God's presence in your life and in the lives of your companions.

Chapter Two

Begin this session with one of the two "living process" exercises, noted on page 51.

1) How do you understand God's power in your life and in the world?

2) How do you understand the power of prayer? Do your prayers make any difference to God?

3) How do you understand the causes of sickness and tragedy? What role does God play in health and illness? In what ways is God present in tragedy and pain?

4) What does the following affirmation mean to you - "God is the fellow sufferer who understands?" Do you think God really experiences our pain? In the spirit of Eric Liddell in *Chariots of Fire* – "God made me fast, and when I run, I can feel God's pleasure" – do you think God experiences our joy and celebration?

5) Where do you experience God's presence most fully in your life? Where do you experience divine possibilities inviting you to new adventures?

Conclude with a time of prayerful contemplation, followed by prayers for group members, the community, the world. Conclude each prayer sentence with the call and response:

Voice One: God in all things

Group Response: All things in God.

Chapter Three

If possible, adorn your meeting space with pictures and artifacts from other faith traditions along with Christian symbols.

Begin your time together with taking time to breathe in God's spirit in light of the wisdom of Psalm 150:6, "let everything that breathe, praise God." Invite participants to breathe deeply the spirit of God in their own lives and then imagine the breath of God spiraling outward as they exhale to include; the persons in the room, the community, the nation, the planet, and the mystery beyond and then back to each one's gentle inhaling of divine energy and wisdom.

1)   How do you respond to the experiential and perspectival orientation of postmodernism? What role do you think "doctrine" plays in the life of faith? In what ways are doctrines important? In what ways are they relative?

2)   Using the metaphor of the running elephant, what "parts" or "aspects" of the divine did you focus on as a child? What "aspects" did you focus on in your teenage or young adult years? What "aspects" of God do you focus on today? What images of the divine have you neglected in your spiritual journey?

3) Do you think there is an "essence" (or one "main trait" of Christianity) or is Christianity multi-faceted? What might be the "essence" or what "facets" do you deem important in Christianity?

4) Do you think faith-traditions "grow" like persons? In what areas do you see Christianity growing as it encounters other faith traditions?

5) As you look at the Christian-Jewish scriptures, what passages are most definitive of your faith? What parts of the Bible might you wish to neglect or eliminate from scripture?

6) What persons of other faith traditions, or no tradition at all, have influenced your life? In what way have they deepened your practice of Christianity?

7) What do you think of the notion of "good enough" revelation or "good enough" scripture? Do you think we can sustain our faith with "good enough" rather than "perfect" in terms of scripture and revelation? Can we live boldly without depending on absolute truth?

Conclude with a time of silence, followed by prayers of gratitude for persons who have helped us find meaning and healing.

Chapter Four

Begin your time together with a few minutes of silence. Then, take time to read a healing story; for example, the woman with the flow of blood (Mark 5:25-34); the man let down from the roof (Mark 2;1-12);or the Syrophoenician woman and her daughter (Mark 7:24-30) in the spirit of "lectio divina" or "holy reading." A simple pattern of lectio divina involves: 1) listening to the story twice, 2) taking a few minutes of silence in which you listen for God's inspiration through the words of scripture (a word, image, or creative thought), and 3) sharing with the whole group your insight, recognizing the "democracy of revelation" through which God inspires each person in the group.

1) How do you understand the uniqueness of Jesus? What aspect of Jesus' ministry is most important to you?

2) Do you think Jesus is the only path to salvation? What is the relationship of Jesus to other "savior" figures in the world's religious traditions?

3) If you were asked to share the meaning of the Jesus' life with another person, what is the most important truth to share about Jesus' life? What is the meaning of Jesus' death for you?

4) How do you understand the miracles and healings of Jesus? Could they have happened in the first century? Can they still happen today?

5) Where do you see the need for Jesus' healing in our world today? Where might you need God's healing touch in your life?

Conclude with a time of prayer for one another. Following each prayer request in the spirit of the bidding prayer from Session Three, say "God in all things" and respond with "All things in God."

Chapter Five

Begin today's session with the "living process" exercise, described on page 95. Then take time as group to read Acts 2:1-12 twice in the spirit of "lectio divina" as you awake as a group to the personal and group inspiration of God's spirit. What words, images, and experiences emerge as you read these words. After a time of conversation, sing Jim Manley's "Spirit of Gentleness."

1) When have you experienced the lively movements of Spirit in your life? When have you experienced the movements of God's Spirit in congregational worship? In both cases, how would you describe your experience?

2) What are your responses to contemporary "faith healers" such as Benny Hinn and Oral and Richard Roberts and to Pentecostal phenomena such as "speaking in tongues" (glossalalia)? Is it possible to be progressive theologically   and   also   experience   the   lively

unexpectedness of God's presence in the life of the church?

3) What words do you use to describe God's nature – publicly and privately? What new words might you imagine using to describe the wondrous complexity of God? Do you feel comfortable using both masculine and feminine language for God in worship?

4) Consider the interplay of the *kataphatic* and *apophatic* orientations in theology and religious experience. What objects and rituals most fully convey God's presence to you? Where do you find God most mysterious?
5) Have you experienced God's presence outside the realm of human religion and experience? Do you think God "speaks" to non-humans? If so, how might God inspire your companion animals and other creatures?

6) Prayerfully read Acts 2:42-47. What words inspire you? How might living in the spirit of this passage transform your faith community?

7) How do you imagine the Trinity? Does the Trinity play any role in your understanding or experience of God? Do you think God is limited to just three manifestations or can you imagine a multitude of other manifestations of God?

Conclude by breathing the spirit deeply as a group, while you take hands with one another. Ask the group to imagine God's spirit flowing in and through the group and then beyond the group into the world.

Chapter Six

Bring photos from the Hubble telescope or other photos of the cosmos to your gathering. Invite participants to experience these photos in silence, following the process of "lectio divina" as explored in the previous sessions. Let the photographs invite persons to explore how God is speaking to them. Invite persons to share words and images that are evoked by these photos of cosmic creation and intergalactic adventure.

1) What is your image of God's creative activity in the universe? Do you think God plays a role in the evolutionary process?

2) Theologians have articulated two primary approaches to divine creation – "creation out of nothing" and "creation out of chaos" or "continuous creation" (God creates in relationship with materials that have power of their own). In light of these approaches to divine creation, how do you understand God's creation of the universe?

3) Traditional theology sees the sin of Adam and Eve as the source of pain and suffering in the world. Process theology sees creation as a call forward bringing forth new forms of life, both good and imperfect. How do you

understand the origin of suffering in the universe? How should we best respond to the pain of the world?

4) How do you understand the relationship of faith and science? Are they antagonistic, complementary, or related to different intellectual worlds? In what ways should we encourage scientific exploration? What limitations, if any, should we place on scientific exploration (for example in the area of cloning or stem cell research)?

5) What role do we as humans have in the future of the universe? Do you see humans as partners with God in the creative process of healing the planet?

For the closing prayer, invite participants to sing an updated and re-translated version of "How Great Thou Art," "O Mighty God, When I Survey in Wonder." (New Century Hymnal, page 35)

Chapter Seven

After a moment of silence, prayerfully read I Corinthians 12:12-27. Then gently invite the participants to participate in the "living process" spiritual exercise described on page 115-116.

1) As you look at your congregation or the church, where do you see God's presence and gifts?

2) While the church's calling is to preach "good news," where have you found the church a messenger of "bad news" to certain persons or groups? In what ways might we more fully participate in the healing of the church?

3) In the body of Christ, there are many gifts. What gifts do you see in yourself? In what ways might we nurture our gifts for service? In what ways might we as members of Christian community nurture the gifts of others?

4) Jesus promised, according to John's Gospel, that his followers would embody "greater gifts" in their ministries than he himself accomplished. Toward what "greater gifts" is your congregation being called? What "greater gifts" does God have in store for you?

5) Today's progressive church is called to embrace the spirit of the German "confessing church." Where is the church called to speak out against our cultural values and political actions? What actions is the church called to take in its role as an instrument of healing for persons, communities, and the planet?

Conclude with prayers of intercession for persons in the group, their loved ones, and the broader community. Conclude each intercession with "God in all things" to which the participants respond "All things in God."

Chapter Eight

Begin your session with the exercise described on page 129, taking time to experience our unity with the multi-layered environment that supports and encompasses us.

1) Reverence for life is at the heart of process ethics. If non-human life has value and must be respected, on what basis do we decide to sacrifice some value-laden life forms for the benefit of others?

2) What counsel does process theology give for resolving certain "culture wars" issues such as abortion and physician-aided death?

3) Process theology claims that ethical decision-making involves attentiveness to God's aim at beauty and value in the immediate moment and the foreseeable future. In what ways might we become more attentive to God's aim at beauty and complexity of experience?

4) Under what circumstances might you support physician-aided death or self-administered suicide? What limits should we place on the various forms of euthanasia?

5) What guidance does process theology give for issues of economics and social justice? What do you think of the phrase, "live simply so that others may simply live?" How might taking that phrase seriously change our lives?

6) What are the ethical implications of the interdependence of life for issues of foreign relations and national sovereignty?

Conclude this session by reflecting on ways the group can live more simply by decreasing our carbon footprint and making more resources available to persons experiencing famine and malnutrition.

Chapter Nine

Begin your session with one of the practices described on pages 135-136. You can close your eyes and imagine God's energy flowing through you or pray with your eyes open, experiencing God's presence in your companions in the room.

1) What spiritual practices nurture your life? What spiritual practices best reflect your personality type and current life situation?

2) What does it mean to say "God is still speaking?" Where have you experienced God speaking in your life? How does this process of ongoing revelation transform your understanding of Christianity and other religious traditions?

3) What does it mean to "love God in the world of the flesh?" (W.H. Auden) In what ways is caring for your body a spiritual practice?

4) What does it mean to be a "practical mystic?" In what way are mystical experiences and ethical actions related?

5) What role does innovation play in your spiritual life? What new spiritual practices do you see emerging in the 21st century?

Conclude your time together with a time of silence, breathing gently the energy of God, letting it transform your life and the group experience.

Chapter Ten

Begin today's session with a time of gentle breath prayer. Then, take a few minutes to read Acts 10:9-23 (Peter's dream of a banquet of unclean food) in the spirit of lectio divina. After reading the passage twice, invite participants to ponder what words or images emerge from the scriptures. Take time to share the unique insights each member of the group.

1) What is your initial reaction to the word "evangelism?" Where have you seen positive forms of evangelism? Where has evangelism been "bad news" for persons?

2) If God eventually will "save" everyone, what is your primary motivation for sharing the good news?

3) What one belief do you feel comfortable sharing with another person unfamiliar with your faith and congregation?

4) Have you ever experienced evangelism as violent in nature? Have you ever experienced evangelism as relational and affirmative?

5) When have you experienced God's creative transformation in your life? How would you express that experience to another person?
Conclude with a time of intercessory prayer, lifting up persons who are in need of God's healing touch or a greater sense of meaning in their lives.

Chapter Eleven

Begin your session with the reading of Romans 8:38-39, focusing on the passage, "nothing can separate us from the love of God in Christ Jesus our Lord [Savior or Healer]." Ask the group to reflect in silence on realities that are frightening. Invite them to create affirmations in the silence, noting objects of fear and anxiety, and then placing them in the following sentence:

_____cannot separate me from the love of God in Christ Jesus our Lord.

For example," my fears of death can't separate me from the love of God" or "my past mistakes can't separate me from the love of God.

1) How do you visualize life after death? Do you think we will remember this lifetime and those whom we loved?

2) Do you think we spiritually evolve in the afterlife? If so, what do you think the relationship is between this life and the afterlife? What are your thoughts about reincarnation?

3) How do you understand "salvation?" Can persons be saved outside of the Christian tradition?

4) Can there be good behavior without the threat of this and other-worldly punishment? What is your image of "hell?"

5) Do you think there is an end to God's love? Do you think that God abandons persons at death or, in the afterlife, if they fail to grow? What role does judgment play in living and dying?
Conclude the group an ancient Celtic practice, known as the "caim" or "encircling."

Stand in a circle with plenty of room to move about – then using your right hand index or pointer figure inscribe a circle as you turn in a circular fashion. Let the circle be a reminder that we always live in the circle of God's care.

Conclusion

Begin with a time of gentle breathing. Then, follow the spiritual practice described on page 156.

1) As you look at your personal theology and spiritual practices, where do you need to grow? Where does your congregation need to grow?

2) What is your attitude toward the future? Do you despair when you think of the planet's future or do you see signs of hope?

3) What role do humans have in shaping the future? Can we contribute to healing the world by our commitments and actions?

4) When you look at the future of process theology, what role do you see it having in the future? Where does process theology need creative transformation in order to be more faithful to God?

5) In the midst of change, what values and beliefs should we preserve and deepen in our faith traditions? Where do we need to explore new values and beliefs?

6) Conclude with considering the following questions: What has your greatest learning been in the course of this study? Have you experienced any new insights as a result of your participation in this study?

Conclude with sentence prayers, which may involve giving thanks for your new insights and for your partners in this study.

www.ingramcontent.com/pod-product-compliance
Lightning Source LLC
Chambersburg PA
CBHW021400090426
42742CB00009B/942